Songs for my Father

a collection of poems & stories

by Kevin Rabas

A MEADOWLARK BOOK

Songs for my Father

a collection of poems & stories
by Kevin Rabas

Meadowlark (an imprint of Chasing Tigers Press)
P.O. Box 333
Emporia, Kansas 66801
meadowlark-books.com

Kevin Rabas
P.O. Box 274
Emporia, Kansas 66801
krabas3@yahoo.com

Cover, "Bushong Piano," and Author Photos by Dave Leiker
daveleikerphotography.com

Cover Design by Eric Sonnakolb
sonnakolb@hotmail.com

ISBN: 978-0-9966801-1-0

Library of Congress Control Number: 2016937165

Songs for My Father

Lift / 3
Knife with a Lion's Head on the Hilt / 4
Buffaloed / 5
No One Wanted Clocks / 6
(Grand) Father Clock / 7
New Bag / 8
My Old Man / 9
Soldier's Burial / 10
Night I bent our credit cards / 11
Eat Fast / 12
Depress & Turn / 13

New Music

New Guitar / 17
Band Wagon / 18
Mark Lowrey on Piano / 19
On Clapping, Shouting in Between Symphonic Movements / 20
Violin notes slope / 21
Ride on / 22
Bottle Problems / 23
Doc Garland's Daughter / 24
Buddy Bolden's Notes / 25
Night Song / 26
The Last Page / 27
Rehearsal with Myra Taylor / 28
High School Jazz / 29
Dixieland / 30
My Take / 31
Almost Rain / 32
"Bewitched" / 33
Teen Logan Richardson on Sax / 34
My Kind of Dance / 35
Praise Band Drums / 36
Late in the Night (at the Jardine's Jam) / 37

Duty & Money

Debtless / 41
Dead Battery / 42
BOE / 43
Stink / 44
Second Holiday Job / 45
Rent / 46
Photo Booth, Emporia, Kansas / 47
Taco Poems / 48
Alms / 49

Prairie Fire

Stopped at the Edge of the Road / 53
Larry Schwarm shoots the fires / 54
Prairie Fire, Moon / 55
Fire Line / 56
Prairie Hills Course / 57

Broken Down Car

Sea Birds / 61
Autoshop, Twilight / 62
John North Ford—Emporia / 63
'67 Mustang Fastback / 64
Broken Down Car, Bikers / 65

The Literary Circle

The Literary Circle / 69
Old Mountain Inn, Chess / 70
The Next Generation / 71
Box / 72
My words wait / 73
Basketball Fall / 74
Meninger's Visit / 75
When I Return Home, After Divorce / 76
Follow the Breath / 77
Arkansas / 78
Bei Dao Book Arrives / 79

The Great Outdoors

Up in Yellowstone / 83
No amount of sheep leads to sleep / 84
March 10th / 85
When the rain comes / 86
Shepherd's Valley Organic Farm, Americus, Kansas / 87
Muddy Kanza / 88
Joe Versus the Volcano / 89
Fire, Possum / 90

We Lived by the River

Second Date, KC Barney Allis Plaza Statuary / 93
Mother's Day Poem #1 / 94
Mother's Day Poem, 2015 / 95
Tallgrass / 96
Avatar / 97

Childhood & Young Adulthood

When I Shit / 101
Wrestling / 102
Underwater Bag Escape / 103
Old Shawnee / 104
King Fish & Sea Bird / 105
Prom / 106
Rum & Coke / 107
White Plume / 108
Arcade / 109
Kid Recital, Violin / 110

A Storied Life: Short Stories

On Las Ramblas / 113
Apartments in Hawaii / 115
Conferencing in Hawaii / 116
Directions in German / 130
Garland Samson on drums / 131
The Naked People / 134
Calculus II / 136

Dead Battery / 138
Elizabeth: a scrap of our story / 139
Really / 140
The Djembe Drum / 142
Church Teen Drum Jam / 145
Turtles Are Worse / 147
Try-Outs, Swim Team, 1991 / 150
Mike Fell Today / 151
You Went Out Dancing / 153
Pool with Dad / 155
Dear Tamara / 158
Live at the Liberty / 160
Hot Tub / 162
Dry-Mount Press / 164
Blood Brothers / 165
To Mow: A Suburban Cautionary Tale / 166

About the Author / 169

Acknowledgements / 171

Words of Thanks / 173

Songs for my Father

Lift

Father says that when that jobsite bully went to sit
    in the can, in the Johnny on the Spot, the craneman
    got him back. Someone attached the hook to the top
    of the latrine, and up it went, lifted above the site,
    the lolly sloshing as it went, crap and piss splashed up
    and onto that bully's butt, and when that bully opened
    the door, down down down he saw, and shut swiftly
    and sat and shat and shat some more and puked.
"What happened when they put him down," I asked,
and father said, "He had to be sent home."

Knife with a Lion's Head on the Hilt

Father holds a broken knife, tells me
   he's swapped an old stage coach gun
to fix it, knife my mother's father brought back
   from Mexico; on the hilt, *Vaya con Dios*, God speed.

Mother, the mayor's daughter, married a humble
   farmer's son, one whose number was up.
Mayor Luder helped put Pop in a reserve unit
   that, when it came to Nam, didn't get sent.

Dad worked on Jeeps and drove generals around,
kept a black wrench; shine was for civilians.
Dark tools don't flash like a mirror in sun,
mark a mechanic's spot for an unlucky pot shot.

Buffaloed

My father takes the dare,
   tees up and aims for the bull
down-course, at college, in Golf 101,
   and hits it, the tail raised, the chest
puffed, the legs pistons. My father flunks.

No One Wanted Clocks

Kansas City, city of skyscrapers. My father
stops crafting the dark wood casings for old clocks
and walks on site, into the skeleton
of rebar and I-beams that climbs
and scrapes sky, pushes through clouds,
holds the sun, mornings, before it's all up
and above the city of sidewalks and streets
and people, like ant shadows, across blacktop, concrete.
My father has photos of giant bodies of brick and steel,
buildings that shadow the street; he worked his way
into the clouds, carpenter to superintendent,
white hard hat to blue, and at home the clocks
stopped, time went on in my father's pocket watch,
and when he dropped one, that small clock fell a long long ways
into the hole; the building rises, starts from a long drop
of darkness, from a hole deep enough to hold
the whole monstrosity up, full of clay and rock and dirt,
and the piers, like the weights in old clocks, long
and cylindrical, but in this case: cement to concrete.

(Grand) Father Clock

Tick of my father's clock,
   the casing, his,
carved & sanded & stained,
   tock & tick, what's left
of father's heart.

New Bag

My father writes a page a day
   in his jobsite diary
in pencil sharpened by pocketknife.
   The shavings line his trailer floor.
Supers write inside.

Twenty-five years
   in pencil,
and a kid from the office
   shows up with a bag,
says, "Open it." "It's plastic,"
   says my Dad. "What is it?"
"A laptop. Keep your diary in here."
"I don't type," says my Dad.
"You're a smart guy. Learn."
"Old dog, new tricks," says my Dad.

That night, my Dad pulls out
   and over that bag
   with his white pickup truck.
The company sends the same guy
   with a new computer. "Learn."

My Old Man

"This is the third time they've set fire
to my trash cans," my old man says, his first year
teaching in the inner city school. "I'm done."
His boss sits with his feet propped up
on a mahogany desk, some ribs from Gates spread out
on white bread, and says, "Wanna quit?
You gotta put it in writing," and my old man,
in his first year teaching industrial arts, shop, reaches across
that desk and takes a napkin and writes: "I quit. –GCR"

Soldier's Burial

My father's on color guard, raises
   his rifle, shoots. The casket's got a flag
draped over the dark casing that holds
   the body, but Dad notices the flag's caught
at a corner of the casket, held.
   The flag should go folded
to the wife. Quick, my father
   opens his Texas toothpick knife,
swipes off that flag corner.
   All's well, only a small piece
of America goes down
   down into the ground.

Night I bent our credit cards

   in half until they snapped,
Julie goes out dancing
   with her ring off. Morning,
and I find car tracks across
   my father's yard, the garden
knocked down, and a vodka bottle
   in the poppies, all gone.
To my father, like a horse head
   left in his bed; his garden, what he does
after work.

Eat Fast

My father pulls his big, construction worker hand from that bag of LAY'S. Salt and oil dot his fingers, hold to the black hairs on the backs of his hands and knuckles. Finish late at the dinner table, and father would fork some food from your plate into his mouth. Eat fast or eat less. This is how we were taught.

Years later, on TV, we learn about how vegetables and grains are the way, all plant. How what has been processed has been filled with sugar and with corn, how as a country we are eating our way to disease.

My father, who brought home good money from his job at the site, kept us well fed, told us to get "desk jobs," urged us to "study up," fattened, lost his mind slumped in blue TV light. Retired, he tried keeping bees, keeping chickens, growing tomatoes, collecting antique crocks. But in the end, he ate chips. His face placid, the light left his eyes/irises, two blue tubes. He walked slow. His speech slurred. He'd shake your hand and say he loved you. But nothing, nothing held.

Depress & Turn

My father's underwater;
   pills in his gullet
turn him slow;
   ghost, zombie,
he walks, haunts,
   dream-man, shadow-man, messenger
from the purple and the blue.

Songs for My Father

New Music

New Guitar

That winter, I shopped for a guitar.
I visited Chris, who taught at a guitar shop.
We played in a band, Hester & the Jazz Puritans,
and Chris knew what a guitar could do—with chords,
with voice, with a string of arpeggio notes.
He ran his pointed fingers over Spanish guitars, folk Martins,
the black Ibanez and red Gretsch and sea foam Stratocaster.
What would Lisa want? Lisa, who sang songs, hands
on the guitar, for her potted plants, wanted
to play out. Banjo Bob brought a wood Seagull down,
and we knew that was it; $600, and I had that axe in hand,
a surprise for Lisa when she returned through those studio windows
and sat by the board, Rainmaker Steve Phillips with his hands
across the knobs, and Lisa, Lisa with her hands across the neck
and the strings. Her nails short, her voice crisp,
her fingers hot with new touch. How she'd make it sing.

Band Wagon

The guys in blue jeans jumped into the back of the rusty pick-up truck.
Inside, cases that held trumpets, trombones. They said, "Come on,"
and in I hopped, and they pulled away, chucking dust and gravel,
then took to grass and pulled down the hill to the football field,
where, above us, I saw glints of silver up, cutting clouds;
I'd never seen batons, the young women reaching
up with white gloves and plucking metal from sky.
Try-outs had happened. They had a band. But they put a pair
of shiny cymbals in my hands, had me hold out my arms,
fly. I held, and they said, "You'll do," and we took to marching
up and down white lines. All around, the air rumbled:
low brass like thunder, flutes like bird call, trumpets like lightning, drums
like buffalo stampede. What I was in moved like a vast animal,
centipede, a many-footed thing, and when we moved, the ground—
the grass—felt us, came up, held, and fell away,
    like the sand does to the sea.

Mark Lowrey on Piano

Icy, high piano notes, birds
   power-line shuffling; beneath,
icicles cling, water drops caught, held
   in beaded strings; breathe,
and you make white smoke.

On Clapping, Shouting
in Between Symphonic Movements

"Hell yeah! Play it, Raylene,"
   Buford shouts in between movements
at the Walton Arts Center—Fayetteville,
and I too want to stomp and shout;
music shouldn't be held in that silent affluent grip
   the Man has: that hand, that greenback-ful fist.

Violin notes slope
the page, flags
like guttering, dots
like water.

Ride on

Only a few Democrats in this town, and Susan & Jason
have the bumper stickers to prove it, back of
the Ford Ranger, "Kansas Dems," a blue circle.
Every season we gather, eat pizza and fruit salad, share
greens we've carted from Lawrence, next town, blue
town—dot—in red rectangle Kansas; here in Emporia, we
were once Progressive; Wm Allen White ran
against the Klan; I remember coal-colored CJ being called to play
with us at the Methodist church, only under-21 bassist in town,
and the tune goes: "Who's got a robe that's long and white…
Ride on, Ride on," and all I can say is, "I think they mean
the Jesus, and hope they don't mean the others
on horses, with the wicked pointy hats," and we laugh, but not
because we know, but because we fear; something of those old
nights of fire and tall crosses, nooses, runs into land we now walk,
dirt fed by blood, and those damned knotted trees still stand.

*William Allen White ran for governor in 1924 in an attempt to expose the
Klan's prejudices. -*The Emporia Gazette*

Bottle Problems

Ryan's drunk, and Anne has a dark green bottle he's brought, and
she's twisting the corkscrew, and the cork, puffed and torn, won't
come out, and she asks me to help, and I break the bottle lip,
thinking *now no one will drink*, but Anne takes out a cheese cloth
and strains the wine through, purple and blood red through white
fabric, abstract art on cloth, the neck of the bottle bent, an angle, a
lever, she moves our drunk world, and I can see the future in
those wine stains, Ryan back on the bandstand, his big brown
upright bass at his shoulder, humming, lowing, string-singing, and,
like gravel under tires, out comes Ryan's Paris voice, lost a
continent over, but now back, in KC, the cat's holler, the KC wail
and bray turned sophisticate by a night of strained wine.

Doc Garland's Daughter

Doc Garland's daughter touched behind her ears,
   as if putting on perfume, when we raved about her singing
   and her hands over those piano keys:
thin, obsidian Alexandra sang: "the sea,
   the sky, you and I," and we all went underwater
with her, in love with that whiskey warmth
of her voice, her way, her heart, her cloud whisper
   of "thank you, all," when finished;
Doc Garland put his Blackberry on whisper,
on hum, on whir; this night was Alexandra's,
and Doc waited like a monk
for her to sing her second set,
for her lick and needle of fire, song.

*Lines 4-5 quote from "All Blues," lyrics by Oscar Brown Jr.; song by Miles
Davis

Buddy Bolden's Notes

"She wants to make love. I just want to drink," folky Bill
Morrissey sings, short Bill in his cowboy hat. He brays in the
Veeches's living room, picket fence old yellow house, on Mass. in
Lawrence, the blue dot, Bill, what we came for, songwriter who
also plays Buddy Bolden's "Funky Butt," a hat tip to the first
jazzer, coronetist Buddy Bolden leading Mardi Gras, his shiny
horn tipped up—to the clouds, to rain and hail, to madness and
Slaughter, the town he landed in after loving two women; insane,
Bolden never played another note, barber turned musician turned
madman, who pointed to the qualities of light on the bathtub
spigot; that is how he talked, without words, just light, like his
photographer friend who took that only shot of Bolden; only
thing that lasts, that and some tunes passed down, ear to horn, ear
to string; Morrissey plays it now, what he learned, from some
hepcat who passed it to hepcat because no one, no one ever got a
note of what Bolden played down—not on tape, on wax ring, on
cylinder or charcoal marks on paper; what Bolden plays comes
only through the body now: musician body, hands and mouth,
fingers on strings. What you hear tonight, only a few know:
Bolden's notes, his solos: all lost.

*This poem draws heavily on the fictionalized history of Buddy Bolden found
in Michael Ondaatje's novel, *Coming Through Slaughter* (1976).

Night Song
for Lisa

Hunched in the bathroom
   at 1:20 in the morning, the sink counter
   my desk, I'm writing you,
asking you not to give up
   on your voice, your words,
your fingers across guitar,
   its thin strings,
its chortle and moan, its
   fluid howl, like blood-song
   through arteries to heart.
I'm asking you to remember
   how I fell in love—
with your words, voice,
how you dug deep and brought
your stories into night, above
coffee grinder hum
and café chatter, and the sound
of city sirens that carry someone
from this world into another
and bring them back, like Orpheus
   with his lyre. I fell in love
with your voice, your words,
that glimpse into the depths
of your heart, the shadows of your past,
like shapes on sidewalk
at midnight, street lamps our only light.

I'm fine being your
   Eurydice, but
you must sing me back again
   each night.

That Last Page

Two months I practiced
  that high school timpani piece,
had it down, never once looked up.
  On the bus to the judges, Tim says,
"Sorry to say this, bud, but there's no
  double bar there; there's
  another page," and I drummed
my way there: left leg A, right leg D,
  seat ahead of me E, my mind
a blender of beat and note,
  and, in luck, I got a "one."

*"one" or "I": highest score in state music competition.

Rehearsal with Myra Taylor

Myra says, "Play that little
    African groove you do,"
and, in Millie's living room, piano
    along one wall, I cup my palms
and clap the drum, use
    the groove Byrd taught us,
his walls lined with drums,
    djembe one way
to fill and hold a room.

High School Jazz

How the high schoolers struggle
    with their solos—
too quiet, too many notes,
    too few—
16th notes strung up and down a scale,
    the repeated phrase "chili pepper,
    chili pepper."

How I want to say:
"Play your song. Drum it.
    Blow. Let what's inside
come out like a breath cloud
    in November cold—
smoke, soul, what's left
    when the spirit's let out."

Dixieland

I play a regular, monthly gig at Aimee's Coffee (10/Mass, Lawrence), and my wife, Lisa, and I come into town early Saturdays, and I write and read in this well-lit, posh Christian coffee house, Lighthouse, before the gig, 2-5 pm, and today Lisa's watching these health coaching videos, since beyond her day gig as a paralegal she aspires to be a health coach, and is studying online, learning what to eat, and when we get to our table and seats, there's a pianist and a tuba, old guys, and they're oom-papa-ing it up, loud, farting brass and spirited teeth keys, filling the front room with C# farts, the light by the window, Jesus-white, and Lisa says, "Damn, I'll be glad when this frickin' Dixieland's done."

My Take

We tear down. I fold the metal snare drum stand,
    its grasshopper legs folding akimbo and in,
and out into the light shower we go, the violet Lawrence drops
    falling on our backs and on our heads and on our bags,
our shoes squishing as we jog and pop open our trunks,
    and Randy stops me in the alleyway, grounds his amp,
reaches into his pocket and hands me two ones, my take
    from the tips, the jar not very, not very full.

Almost Rain

The rust color of Mass. street brick
   opens, nude to the grey-white sky
before rain, before clouds pour down, black
   on the game goers, the Jayhawkers,
in their shapely blue and red shorts, tees,
     as my wife and I watch
   from the yellow-lit coffee shop,
lighthouse, *Signs*, and drink
   our too-tall teas, grade overdue poems,
papers, think nothing   of the notes
   we'll play, sing   tonight
in another, smaller, darker coffeeshop
   near the park, place that's hosted us,
     once a month, for over a decade, and no one
complains, no one complains about our sound.

"Bewitched"

Icy high notes, eighth notes
in the intro. to "Bewitched," Mark Lowrey's hands
over the keys, solo—a tune I still have trouble listening to,
beginner's tune, singer's tune, along with "Route 66"
and "Feel Like Makin' Love," tune
Tanya sang over and over in the PAC practice room,
a room really only big enough for drums and one other
person, but we're all here—drum and drummer,
Tracy on bass, Chris on guitar, and long blonde Tanya,
who keeps forgetting the words—beautiful Tanya,
who found us practicing late one night
for a gig we played for popcorn before the movies,
classic flicks, "The Robe" and "Ben-Hur," Tanya,
who served drinks at The Cup and Saucer, who studied acting,
but who really, really only wanted to sing, cute Tanya,
who touched Tracy on the arm after a tune, ruffled
his beard, cute Tanya, who has made me hate this tune, until
I hear it again, and almost forget her, as Lowrey plays.

*PAC: Performing Arts Center

Teen Logan Richardson on Sax

Young Logan, in his football jersey, strength
   in bulk, a sax man solid, all muscle, his arms
   like tree branches close to the trunk, plays
fast, fast as you can think, then opens his heart
   like a lineman, like a brick broken open,
like a flower climbing out of a mountain
   crack; *saxifrage splits the rocks.*

*William Carlos Williams: "A Sort of Song"

My Kind of Dance

The DJ spins
  the LP from my time,
Digital Underground's "Humpty Dance,"
  and for one song
I'm not so odd, am
  a regular guy,
swinging one arm, dancing
  as I can, to the beat,
right up on it, not
  all muscles and pecs,
some marching bulldog, but
  just another skinny freak
in the spot, in the cone
  of light, like a man
with plastic glasses and nose,
  burnt as a fry-cook, made
a star by a single funky song.

*Shock G ("Humpty Hump"), an alter ego of musician Gregory Jacobs,
allegedly burnt his nose working as a fry cook, and wears a Groucho Marx style
glasses and false nose.

Praise Band Drums

I.
James scrubs the tub, sings
"Get down with the man
   called Jesus.
   He my Jesus."
Done, he rises
   from his knees.

II.
James imagines Jesus
   stepping from his boat:
"He's the man called Jesus
   in the middle of the water."
He walks   across the blue.

III.
James got fired
   from the church
praise band, makes up
his own words, lyrics
   in the bath, in the shower.

IV.
"We've had complaints
   from the older congregation
   members. They say
   you're too loud on drums."
"How quiet do you want
   me to play," says James, playing.
"Quieter," she says.
"This quiet?" says James.
"Quieter."
   James stops.
"This quiet?"
"Perfect," she says.

Late in the Night (at the Jardine's Jam)
for Mel & Matt

Around 1 in the morning at Jardine's on Main, Paul Waters calls
Mike Karr to the stand, Karr, the best young drummer in this
town, KC, in the early '90s, Karr who works with me at the
MARR Sound Archive, home of over 300,000 classic jazz, blues,
country and pop recordings. We shelve. We soap-bath the LPs.
Karr who wears a ball cap or beret or newsy cap because he's
balding in his late 20s, almost a decade older than me, Karr who
plays with Mohammad's band, only white drummer to since the
'30s, '40s. Karr's a humble white god on skins, on tubs, on drums,
his sticks polyrhythmic, his time steady and groovin' as a night
train's rumble, his soul bright and unusual as the bell of a black
saxophone, Parker's horn.

Karr's downed a few: whiskeys, scotches—comps from ladies
who stand along the bar and pinch a young butt, who dig
musicians more than fast cars; when Karr steps to the tubs, his
legs wobble. Waters calls "Cherokee," then "Little Sunflower,"
and Karr, who can outrun a leopard, a rumble of hi-hat and floor
tom gallop, his hands like Cuisinart blenders across the bright
cymbals and drums, falters, gives up on his slow legs, feet, and
punches the cymbal like a speed bag, his feet under fire, under
frost, under the darkness of hard liquor; he can't hang, and I want
to cry to watch him slow, to hear that space, that silence his feet
keep; his arms, though, his arms can still hit, (almost) fallen hero,
kid with too much brew in his blood.

Songs for My Father

Duty & Money

Debtless

When the loan officer shakes my hand, his hand is a big mitt, ham shank, boxer's big thick grip, and, though he's kindly, he's big, the kindly high school quarterback turned accountant, and he has the talc scent of powder, strong stiff cologne, and new money, greenbacks fresh from the mint, crisp as new printer paper, with that whiplash snap, when you riffle the bills, something never to be felt again: that freedom, that easy going feel, that blank check.

Dead Battery

I called my ex-girlfriend, when my Blazer battery died in the Tune Shop parking lot. Jawaun needed a new thick metal d-string for his bass. We had the hood open, when Bea got there, the jumper cables out and coiled. Bea drove us to the Little Apple Wal-Mart, and we got the battery, undid the screws, and lifted it in—and, on the way back, we all stopped and watched white ruffled couples dance through the window of the old folks home, there in the grass by the curb, Bea's hand in my hand.

BOE

After the election, I go out,
get the *Shopper* from the drive
  in the dark,
pull up my yard sign
and prop it against the washer.

Tomorrow, there'll be plenty
more signs to pull up.

*BOE: Emporia Board of Education race, 2 April 2013:
Crouch: 1590, Windsor: 1584, Epp: 1559, Rabas: 1089

*Shopper: local community news and advertising newspaper

Stink

Downstairs, there's a stink. I flush the pot. The smell's not gone. I look behind the white, porcelain pot at the glue trap, a rectangular box with both sides cut out, a thing for spiders and mice. I nudge the trap with a plunger, use the stick end. The trap's heavy with weight. Looking, I see the reason. There's a little, little mouse, gray. A lump. He's curled for the last time, will no longer eat from the cat's bowl. I sack him in plastic, carry him to the curb. I hope that's the last of him and his. Mice.

Second Holiday Job

Dan (50) works in computers
   at the U, checks us out
at Walmart, aisle 9, needs
more this Christmas, baby
due when the ball falls, kingdom
come, New Year like a bullet,
like an anvil, like a piano
   to the head.

Rent

Mother sends me up to the duplex
   to get the rent
from Crystal, three weeks overdue; mother
   has tired of knocking,
and so I do; 14, and I have a small job
   or two: mowing, magic shows,
rubberbanding the local paper
   for throwing, now this; I knock
and knock. No one comes. Then, a shuffle
   and a rattle, and the lock slides
and springs, and Crystal, 21, stands pale
   and nude, her breasts, doves.
She turns, stoops, and hands me a wad
   of greenbacks, rubberbanded,
and I walk home, erect, awed, and
   I'm scrunched in the corner, when mother
makes the call, red-curled cord stretched
   across the room.

Photo Booth, Emporia, Kansas

That semester away, I walked the mall nights,
   saw movies alone, let the photo booth light
snap me, blank faced, mouth open, to say,
   "I miss you. I won't be home, but I'm here,
making us some money, finding us a way
   into this town." In the best shot, my hand
is at my temple, thinking
   about how to curve the class,
make more B⁺s and A⁻s,
   how to keep my job and start
some poets, grow the language,
   let them feel the page, and make me
whole, know the world is worth
   every word, every silence, every distance.

Taco Poems

I. Tortilla Jack's

Choose four hard corn tacos
   in plain white butcher paper
over some white flour, drip-through
   soft tacos kept warm downtown under a lamp
with a hot orange bulb.

Choose the land of dark hardwood interior
over the land of teal plastic.

Choose the conversation of graying grade school soccer
   coaches over the chatter of slick SUV travelers—
iPhones out—who stop only at the chains.

II. Cheap Tacos

Walk across from the college
   and get four tacos and a drink
for $5.07 on a weekday.
   Less weekends.
See flecks of history painted in brick.
TORTILLA JACK'S
The letters crack in rain and wind.

Alms

Pastor Stan tells me he thinks the church should serve the poor more.
Forget welfare, the church should do its work. Pastor Stan holds
up his nose. Allergies? A Californian, all of Kansas
causes sniffles, snot. His wife stays inside, homeschools.
They put up an orange cone, let the kids
have the drive and yard. "Someone told me that trick,"
says Stan. "Put a cone where your drive meets the street.
Slows folks." A student of mine who's lived in the woods,
spent tent nights, tells me she's getting married. They don't
have much, stop off at Stan's church for pantry food. Christine
tells me Pastor Stan had her wash church windows for her food.
"You've got to work," she says he said. "Earn your food."
Christine goes home, eats ramen noodles with her groom. He rubs
her hands, rubs her feet. She sleeps. Her husband rises and works
a double. They honeymoon between shifts.

Songs for My Father

Prairie Fire

Stopped at the Edge of the Road

Papa stops the pick-up at the edge of the road,
  and we watch the black smoke overtake blacktop.
Some cars troll through, headlights like yellow discs,
the smoke like a swarm of dark insects that leave dark trails.
Papa steps from the cab and holds my hand.
I'm 9. We stand by the fire, a drizzle of yellow
and red, a fringe at the edge of a long black dress.
The cars lumber through. From the wheel,
the farmer men raise one finger or two, a wave.
Fifteen, thirty minutes and it's through, the fire
snuffed at the fringe of the breakdown lane.
Some smoldering smoke, but the swarm's moved on,
and the clouds are now black above, and we can
see into the flint hills, the road a grey ribbon
threading grasslands black with renewal and soot.

Larry Schwarm shoots the fires

Larry drops an L-shaped camera back
on his way to the truck; the flames come:
a wave, a line of yellow-red fingers, and burn
that camera back, the metal: fireplace black, cracked.
Larry sends the camera part to the camera company
with his weekly shots of the fire, and they send him
a new one, untouched by the small hands of fire.

Prairie Fire, Moon

June, and the tan tallgrass fire is high
 as a man's waist, black tree limbs like bones
from ground: leafless, jointed. The moon
like an eye that can only watch and wait
as the prairie burns and lifts a cloud
to block out twilight, like the lift
of ten hundred starlings.

Fire Line

The grasslands, a charcoal black smudge
with a line of yellow-red at the edge, fire line
drawn by the hand of a child: uneven,
but with fierce, ragged symmetry: butterfly wings
of flame. The cars slow, the smoke comes up in rolls
that roil over the breakdown lane, grey-black
waves, up at the fringes like spirits, tendrils,
fingers: last breaths of the tallgrass
up and up into the black clouds above.

Prairie Hills Course

Hank Jones hauls by the bucketfuls
the black pock-marked eggs, the golf balls
that made it out of the range and into the prairie
and were rolled over by flames, when the country course
was windswept at the edge by fire, a fringe
of late June red and yellow, fire high as Hank's waist.

Songs for My Father

Broken Down Car

Sea Birds

My car's radiator broken, the engine overheat light on,
   we pull off the road and look at the ocean,
     two young Kansans on vacation, nearly to New Orleans.
Bea says, "Look at those birds," and our eyes swift
   to the grey-tipped terns, their wings lazy Vs,
they drift on the winds above the white-capped sea.
   They float, and our hands come together, clasp,
as if taken together by wind, and our troubles dissolve,
   like sugar into water, and I tell Bea, if the radiator
catches on fire, I'll take our patch-work quilt, douse
   it in our jug of water, smoother, and, like that,
the fire of our lips is doused with a kiss.

Autoshop, Twilight

Hour
when the autoshop slows, stops,
   (hats off, tools down),
when the mechanic's son
plays with a ball in the lobby, hour
when the lights snap off,
keys come out, and the well cars are all sent home.

John North Ford—Emporia

Below the sign ("collision repair
  front office"), a fenced-in cage
of bumpers + hoods + driver side,
  passenger side doors,
bent + crumpled + upended:
  blacktop of smashed glass.

'67 Mustang Fastback

I.
Gene says, "How fast can she go?" and I use
   his detector to spot cops, and crank the car up,
and she goes 110, and we almost run out of gas
   on the way back to town.

II.
Erica plants a kiss on my driver's side window, leaves.
   She loves my car. Night, my hair
full of pool water, I open my door, touch
   the pink lipstick print, wonder, "Will she ever kiss me?"

Broken Down Car, Bikers

When Kim comes, he brings his guitar, sings,
and when we ask about his father,
    about that motorcycle gang that came in a cloud
    of dust, the Stafford family car stopped,
    hood full of smoke, and that rumble of engines
    and spokes and chrome like pulled
    knives; Kim says father stood,
    like a stone, like a monk, like a man
who can say: *Nothing. Nothing here. Move on*,
    and the day clears of its clouds,
and the cycle gang rumbles past. They look;
don't stop. Their taillights glint, blink red.
Their tires pull dust clouds. Gravel, like a gnash
of cracked teeth, and the clouds
    follow them down the road.

Songs for My Father

The Literary Circle

The Literary Circle

At the Writer's Den, people dressed well, had on suits and sports jackets and slacks and ties, had blouses that were slick and shimmered. Ron with his monk-cut hair, bald on top, his body willow-slender, held his wine glass in one hand and swung his other; his mind was there, with that hand, in the air—and what Ron said could be said to be literature, if someone were to write it down. You might do well to parrot what Ron said the next time you held wine. But Liz and me, we drank Jack in the park afternoons, and we wanted so badly to be "in." When we came in the door, only a few of the affluent looked up, and at that not long. They went back to their talk and their wine. Their club was utterly complete without us, and, without us, they would go on.

Old Mountain Inn, Chess

Fayetteville, Arkansas, 1995

That night, I played chess in a coffee shop in the square,
  the table top, bric-a-brac pieces of glass and clay
  mortared or glued together; the man I played,
  homeless, beat me soundless in 10 moves, smiled
  with bent and broken teeth, some like brown, thin rods,
  no longer white or shaped like ice, but now
  like lo mein twigs; he rubbed his chin,
    and I bought him an Americano and a muffin, gave him
    $5 for the lesson, and he taught me to castle, how to change
    the rook for the king, an easy move, but all I'd ever learned
    were what patterns the pieces made: the bishop's diagonals,
    the queen's long clean lines, the knight's L-shaped hop;
that night, I climbed to the top of the Old Mountain Inn,
  opened an unlocked door, and peered in at that trance
  sect, Maharishi Mahesh Yogi's tribe,
  The Beatles gone, prophet gone, but the people
  still here, the inside of the walls of the hotel now overtaken
  with fica, and in the halls, men and women in orange drapes,
  hands in their laps, singing, praying, sleeping in lotus;
  to join them would be to step into a cloud
  and touch lightning, put a hand to the outlet, jump
  from the conscious to subconscious, when what I really needed
  was to learn how to move the pieces, to touch and hold
  and advance; days of dreaming done, what I'd come
  to Arkansas to do was to write, and, as long as I could hold
  a pencil, pen I would. Notebooks filled afternoons.
  Classes days. The Africa man taught us
  how a lion snaps a man's neck with one quick slap;
  go and learn something about life, then write.
My RA said, "Reading, writing, that's kind of like
  sleeping, isn't it?" No, I said, it's like being jolted
  straight awake by thunder, lightning.

The Next Generation

Nate draws a turtle, who smokes, on the green
blackboard, presents on Bob Marley. William
was Nate's great uncle, uncle who got orange cylinders
of pills, samples, for Christmas. Nate works
construction summers, painting, roofing,
comes home with poems, loads of loud words
echo, like a nail gun, in his head. I play drums
for class, run video, sing poems, tell Nate: Keep at it!
Poems run in your family. What the river says,
you, too, can say. Let the words stream through you—
catch them, take them, when they come.

Box

Outside, it's raining ice. Inside, I
   put my socks on, type. Until the power
goes out, we work. Until there's no light,
  we watch: the TV, the screen, the book.
There's no rest for us. We do not watch
   the rain, the snow, the sun that comes
in through the windows yellow at sunset.
   We do not watch the kids play
football in the street. Ours is a life
   of screens: photos, a few words,
   a string, a feed, a dis list.
Someone else's life in a box
   that we watch from our box,
feel right at home.

My words wait
on your coffee table while you sleep
    on your couch or in your easy chair,
bathed in blue tube TV light; I'm here with you.
A book is a slow thing, a prayer,
    a diary page, a conversation
    already over, a plot
    you'll never need, words
that depict where you once lived
    or wanted—and how;
every love you've ever remembered
    and some you haven't—

—a green worry stone the size
    of your thumb;
a blue rabbit's foot; your first
    love letter, her blue
    pen loops—and hearts drawn
    over all of the I's;
the sway of the candle's flame,
    as if the yellow fire moved
to your apartment's music
    as you made love
    that first time;
the black skeletal trees in winter,
    and their thick coats of snow,
    their bend, their creak, their snap,
    how they go—with a smooth blonde wound
    and knives, knives all around.

Basketball Fall

When I fell,
I jumped back up, blood
in my brain, and played out the game.
I missed every shot, couldn't hit
that red box right, nor the rim,
nor swish net, everything just
a little off, or more.
This tall guy who knocked me down, his friend
kept shoulder checking me, setting picks,
and I'd hit & hit & hit, go soft, step back.
He even clenched a fist, and I said, "Let's end
this," and he backed down, let me by. I was 25.
Truly, some of me never left that pick up game,
those blonde boards. Coaches say, "Leave it all
on the court," and I left my easy smile,
each laughing net, that pink crinkle
around my lips, that breezy walk.

Menninger's Visit

I.
Alicia brings me
   a copy of Sylvia Plath
and a deck of playing cards, visits
me at Menninger's. Alicia: "She, too, cracked."

II.
I consider breaking a window, jumping.
Consider going over the fence, during
smoke break, the lawn cart
chasing me, one fat orderly
   at the wheel, another
   on the CB, black pocked box
to his lips, catching spit.

III.
Night, and they take the bulbs.
You can cut yourself with 40 watt light,
see truth, write bright.

IV.
The pills in the miniature paper cup
   cut at my gut, do not lead
   to sleep, but a cloud,
a cloud of sunken days.

When I Return Home, After Divorce

Mom: See those bees out by the railing? Young bees. Orienting themselves. They go out and back to the hive. Out and back. First, they buzz around the hive, look around, so they know where to return.

Follow the Breath

Mother loads the VHS tape into the TV.
   I'm on the couch. She says, "Rise,"
and I do. We watch a man
   in yoga pants on the beach, the white sun
like a klieg light, the man's goatee long
   and gray and thin, like an Egyptian's, and he raises one leg
then swishes it outward, his leg, his foot: a wave,
   his hands, a dove near his chest. I'm learning tai chi
in the dark in my parents' house, having been
   knocked down in a pick up basketball game, bleeding
in the brain; my wife moved back
   to her parents', too; learn, relearn
now how to breathe.

Arkansas

Jim pulled the pipe from his mouth with a grey cloud puff,
    said, "You're a long shot, kid." The guy I'd come
to study with was in Amsterdam, on sabbatical, and here I was,
    my things all in one truck, everything, and the school
I'd landed at said I was out of luck, nothing here for you.
    They said I could take undergrad classes and beg my way
into a form and structure grad class, maybe take
    an upper level UG class in fiction writing
with the white man back from Africa, and I stayed,
    played jazz drums with the band, which offered
me a small scholarship to stay and play, but I left, pages
    in my wake, read poetry at nursing homes, tried to put
my head back on straight. I thought I'd lost it all
    in Arkansas. I was no longer shocked at the silver shells
at the side of the road, the armadillos, that jump
    right before the bumper comes, an impulse
to make those crawlers seem big, one that makes them
    flat, blood across the road, tire marks across
their small small backs.

*UG: undergraduate

Bei Dao Book Arrives

The Bei Dao book comes, a translation, and his voice arrives from China, like cobalt rain, like motorcycle hum, like moonlight shimmer on blacktop oil pool slick, so city, nature up from cracks and in puddles and atop rooftops, pigeon wings and orange-pink feet, and here, in this little Midwestern city, the glass blowers trade breath with metal pipes, with sand heated 'til it glows, lit like the mountain-center fire, magma, lightning at tree-center, what we see, here, in Kansas, when the anvil-headed storms come like freighters, like battleships, and drop water-rocks on rooftop on field of undulating, crisp, fragile, hops-colored, hard winter wheat, and batter-down-droop all of our crops.

Songs for My Father

The Great Outdoors

Up in Yellowstone

That summer,
Mother drove me to Yellowstone
to see my sister, the ranger;
a lap full of paper, I wrote
while she drove, filled
a one-inch notebook. Left
my wife in Belton, who went
out dancing with her ring off. I went
underwater in the trailer tub, stayed
under until I could cry no longer.

An old buffalo
wallowed outside the metal
walls in dirt. We stayed in.
I knew what it was to leave
and rejoin the herd.

"my sister, the ranger": My sister, Alicia, was an interpretive ranger stationed at Canyon in Yellowstone National Park.

"leave and rejoin the herd": Many male buffalo eventually leave the herd.

No amount of sheep leads to sleep. Like sheep, my mind wanders off, turns red hot, follows thought, how number leads to number in white chalk, how rules of calculus never end, $\tau = \mu \, dv/dy$, how a drop of rain turns to tomorrow's river, and numbers follow, down down down into the sea.

RE: flow of water: where τ is the stress, μ is the viscosity, and dv/dy is the velocity gradient

formula provided by Dr. Christopher Pettit, Physics Professor, Emporia State University

March 10th

70 out, and I'm in my Birkenstocks at 2
in the afternoon, the neighborhood quiet,
except for birds, call and chirp, my forehead
pinks in spring sun, warms
and brightens like the skin of new fruit.
A rabbit rustles
    in last fall's leaves.

When the rain comes,
   last fall's tan and rust-colored leaves
toss along the sidewalk, asphalt,
   first drops, and everything moves, flees,
before the sky drops buckets, blankets,
   drops last week's drink
from ponds.

Shepherd's Valley Organic Farm, Americus, Kansas

The green rows stretch
  out an acre long,
in each row something new.
  When I go
to pick up our share,
  the tabby country kittens
climb onto my office khakis,
  leave little mud pad spots, snags.

Although you can drive
  in any direction five minutes
and see fields, who does?

Muddy Kanza

Derailer off, mud caked
   through the chain, tires
like donuts, they carry
   their bikes
over the mud
   & rough.

Emporia, KS, 30 May 2015

The Dirty Kanza, in Emporia, KS, is the 200-mile premier gravel and road race.
The night before the 2015 race we received heavy rain.

Joe Versus the Volcano

Patricia says, "I love you!" and Joe says, "I love you, too…
   but the timing stinks. I've got to go," and they jump
into the volcano, together they fall
   and fly. And as the towers go down, two people
also made a couple by fire, concrete and steel
   buckling beneath, jump, fall.
And maybe they never hit,
   just fall into smoke, into clouds
brought down by two planes
   brought down by two planes.

Fire, Possum

Night we're tested to sleep outside with no tent, just a bag on the ground and that fire we've made from sticks, a possum with his pinking shear teeth wobbles up to my little yellow fire; spittle drips from his needle-fine teeth, and foam froths from the crook of his grin, perhaps rabid, and I think quick, pull the fuel-rich mosquito repellant dropper bottle from my front jeans pocket and spray the stream into the fire's center, and up shoot the flames, full of "strong medicine," full of alcohol, spunk, and that tall-flamed flash fire spooks our possum, who turns, white-pink tail, a trail, a pale snake into the pitch, into the circle of hickories and tall tree shadows that define night.

We Lived by the River

Second Date, KC Barney Allis Plaza Statuary

Lisa crouched down and looked at the statues'
  little dicks. I took pictures.

One shot is Lisa's album cover—
just Lisa's face, the statue cropped out—
Lisa's little grin, October wind;
she's at play with her new boy in the city.

The plaza is peopled with statues—
stone men, stone women:

Dionysus rises up
with his naked babes;
hands up, they adore,
but never catch him.

Sad faces on a pale pillar stick
out their tongues: spit, dribble.

A stone boy pees into a pool. A stone
frog watches.

Danae takes off her clothes
on the corner of Nichols and Brush Creek.

Mother's Day Poem #1

We lived by the river, and our son
   would drop stones into the water.
Out back, we planted a willow in the corner
   of the chain link, and that tree drank the water
   that would pool when it rained.
At night, we curled into each other
   on a bed that whispered with trees;
   their branches pawed softly at our roof.

Mother's Day Poem, 2015

At age 11, E is part boy, part teen, and he
   pets your arm, rubs noses, hugs;
     he loves his mama.

Beside you, on the couch,
   he learns physics and love
from the blue tube; he laughs at Sheldon, moves
   his arms like a robot, learns
the equation for affection
   from Leonard and that gang sprawled
on the couch with take-out, with chopsticks,
   with food in their laps, and you laugh,
     tossle E's hair.

*Sheldon Cooper and Leonard Hofstadter, characters from the TV show *Big Bang Theory*.

Tallgrass

for Lisa

That afternoon, you wore white underthings that go underneath a
wedding dress, and we sat in the window, sun coming in the little
bed & breakfast that led to the plains, tallgrass just 10 minutes by
car, and we locked hands and walked in the sun, your back
reddening; my camera out, I snapped shots of you eying the sun,
the trail of your white beaded wedding dress like the fringe of the
sea, and what our water was, blonde blonde tallgrass, sister of
seagrass, when this was all once underwater, when what we'd do
now, had we lived thousands of years ago, is swim, your hair like
a seafan, my hands like fins, your legs like a blue-green mermaid
tail, holding, holding us up.

Avatar

Eliot finishes his cereal and says, "Love you, mama,"
  places his spoon in his bowl and walks it all to the counter,
then leaves for his bath says, "Come soon, mama."
  All he wants to do is talk, tell you his day,
how his hands on the keyboard, moved pixilated men,
  stacked MINECRAFT block upon block, a life
of dreams, bits, and color; his avatar, with sword and shield,
  runs circles around noobs and jocks and freaks,
and stows what he's left within chests, tells you
  of his fights and fails, and says little of his life
within skin, feet in dirt, hands wrapped around a bat, other life,
  child life; in the game, he's already grown.

Songs for My Father

Childhood & Young Adulthood

When I Shit

At school today, I start toward a restroom, but stop. A fat, bullyman who oversees the university food is going in. He turns my stomach. I head toward another Men's Room, but a cleaning person has the door blocked with a stick, a big bucket of water near the door, and a mop.

I like to shit alone. Years ago, in grade school, the bigger kids would pin us in the stalls, beat us, or rattle the doors, while we held, while we prayed, while we crimped our fists.

That stays with me, and I wish to be alone, am very very quiet when I sit, shit.

Wrestling

Patrice said Earl had been pickin' cotton, pulling crotch hairs; this
when we'd come out of the locker room, in our all-whites: tee,
shorts, socks; everybody the same for Spoofnagle, short, wrestler-
built, age 35 or so, with those high high tight gym teacher shorts:
his keys in his front pocket, wrestling with the fabric to get free,
but held by the pocket as if by an infant fist; Spoof says nothing,
lets us jibe and jab and cuss each other; even lets us kick, punch
each other; not his business, he says through his uneven smile, his
arms across his chest; he teaches us to kip-up, to lie on our backs
and spring up, a wrestler move, right and fight; it's hard to do,
even for seventh graders; I'm 5'9", 120 pounds, a bean pole; grew
7 inches in one year; and my arms are wrapped like a pretzel,
round me, when the bigger guys get me into the ring; what I know
of wrestling I learned on the shag floor or on a bed at a cousin's
house, wrestling Ben to sit next to cousin Sarah, who's fine, has
blonde ringlet locks; incest is lost on us, and we don't even touch
or kiss, but a girl's a girl, and we fight over her. Earl's skinny like
me, smart, chocolate colored, like Patrice, though Patrice is
darker, mows in the sun summers, tans darker black; I'm white,
from the suburbs, but lower suburbia; my dad works construction,
wants us smart, says, "Get you an office job, kid. Don't go like
me," and I don't know what he means, but I know he swings his
arms wide, proud, simian-like, when he walks, like a man who's
walked out of a German forest into another of rebar and concrete
forms, the building going, going up.

Underwater Bag Escape

That summer I lifeguarded, sat in the stand. Geoff said, "Throw him into the pool in the bag and see if he gets out." I had been practicing magic— that trick, that escape, and knew someone would see, would understand my plan to cheat water, cheat breath, cheat sand, cheat cheer girl curves and lineman muscle; skinny I'd still find a way to shag, be magical, mystical, a young Copperfield or Blackstone, sexy, airless, weightless, immortal, be six-packed Houdini, grab lock picks and needles with my eyelashes, in a back bend, uncuff myself, free myself, unlock, unpack, rise and sail over the audience in a puff of smoke, be a black cloud, silver cloud, a blue cloud, nail-biting wonder; rise like Tesla's lightning, and arc and strike in all directions, tree-limbed shaped and bright white and orange neon thunder; my voice, God's voice, his breath, spectral; my way, the water's way; my death, a choice.

Old Shawnee

I return home to see my parents
   & the old neighborhood,
the paint flaking, & the quarter-million
   houses gone in, shadowing
the $65K ranches of the '70s, my parents'
   place, the pond & cattails gone,
gone the cottonwood four stories high, & the cows
   that would come up to the baby pool, and we'd round them up
& away, whistles round our necks, the cow flanks
   like hot rocks in Kansas sun; Shawnee, little old
Shawnee, first KC suburb, now gone large & greenback green,
   rectangle boxes sprung up 'round everything old;
Garrett's grocery with those slabs of meat hung
   at the back, and with buckets out front
for spent Coke bottles,
   a nickel, one whole nickel, each.

King Fish & Sea Bird

Dad talked to an old man at the dock,
   who uncoiled a frayed rope
and took us out on his boat, early.
   My sister went green, laid her cheek
to the boat's floor. Mother helped
   father string the bait, little fishes
used to catch bigger fishes, the line
   in the water straight, white, skipping
like for skiing. I was ten, and caught
   a king fish. The old man pulled a stick
with a metal point, hauled the fish, big
   as a baby pool, up to the side
of the boat. The line snapped, and that fish
   dove with a flop and a splash, and the lines
in my father's face deepened. We'd lost
   the big fish. But in the wind a bird
came by and lit on my father's shoulder,
   a sea bird, white as a dove, and my father
smiled, pleased.

Prom

Kara's father shoots video of me and his daughter, her dress
seafoam green and blue, my bowtie the same, our cheeks pink,
love-flushed.

Kara's Dad's camera is new, and so, by mistake, he shoots the
whole night on its side, our feet to the left of the frame, our heads
to the right, aslant, and when we drive off, my car shoots up like a
rocket, blasts off.

Rum & Coke

Audra said she was the daughter of a nun.
  Sometimes, we fall hard. We drank rum
and Coke from porcelain coffee mugs,
  watched BBC comedies, 1-3
in the honors dorm, and when I was too drunk
  to stumble home, she lent me
her roommate's bunk, and I slept
  in her room, watched her chest fall
and rise in the purple night, gazed
  at Dali's clocks on a poster,
and we never touched, but slept
  it off. In the morning, I took my coat
and left in the yellow light. I even left
  that mug, so much better than a red
Solo cup, the taste of Coke and rum
  still thick on my tongue.

White Plume

The Brinkmans and my family battle a giant crab.
  He's got a copper amulet round his arm (vs magic),
and he swings his pinking shear claws and clips
  my wife's character's shoulder, and she howls.
We all sit around the kitchen table and roll dice
  and move pencils over paper, tally points.
My son invents three magic weapons,
  including a dagger that sings. Treasure, he says.
The Brinkman kid stands and shouts
  his character's moves; his cleric swings
his silver mace, cures wounds. There is
  no darkness in this dungeon, only light.

White Plume Mountain is a classic Dungeons & Dragons module/adventure.

Arcade

After the summer swim meet
   we get pizza as a team, play
the arcade in our hoodies. A girl looks over
   my shoulder as I toggle, as I button-
mash, as I steer a little man or ship
   into his future, or doom; I keep going,
the game dinging, and she watches,
   her face a pale ghost in the black screen,
watching, unspeaking; I wish she'd put
   her hand on my arm or on my shoulder
or rest her head on me, as I battle light.

Kid Recital, Violin

for Tara

The kids bow in starts and fits;
the pianist must rush to keep up.
As with mad Vronsky and his horse,
kids push and pull until
the pianist's digits bend, bow.

*In Tolstoy's *Anna Karenina*, the affluent cad Vronsky pushes his horse beyond its limit in a race and breaks his horse's back.

A Storied Life:
Short Stories

On Las Ramblas

for Solamon

On the beach in Barcelona someone stole my shoes and knapsack. Inside was all my cash. I had some credit cards under my t-shirt on a travel lanyard, but I'd never used the cards to get cash and couldn't figure out the Barcelona ATMs. I found a pair of notched and chipped drumsticks, one without a tip, outside a club and pieced together a street kit, using an empty milk carton, cardboard, tin cans, and a Snapple bottle, and joined a busking jazz trio. I'd played jazz in KC. Almost paid my rent. I also worked at a jazz archive, shelving LPs.

We played on Las Ramblas, Barcelona's party street, similar to Canal Street in New Orleans, alongside Elvis impersonators, mimes, chalk artists, jugglers, and fire breathers. The fire breathers hated us. We were in their spot, and in the twilight we were gathering steam. Seeing the junk I was playing, young American and European guys sidled up with their travel drums—dumbeks and tablas—their hands quick but boxy, straight 8th players. Squares.

Our bearded bassist, Lars, squinted his eyes and spat. "We're not payin' you all to sit in," and we didn't. But they stayed anyway, angering the fire breathers because where there's a pool of guys grooving, fanboys and hipster chicks will drop change, and our white plastic bucket kept chanking and thumping, so full it no longer wobbled in wind on dark brick.

The fire breathers paced in front of us, cutting the crowd, in gypsy pants. The man, shirt off and tan, with muscles like a boxer's, cat-thin and quick, had leather bands tied below his biceps. He'd chug liquor and spit, light the spray, poof-cloud fire. A woman dressed in pastel scarves like Jeannie Dream paced and sometimes lit his spits or stuck a short lit stick down his throat.

No one noticed them much, and so, when the hip traveler kids on hand drums went into a shout-chorus frenzy, clamping shut their eyes, reddening their fingers, Jeannie Dream kicked our white change bucket over. Little tattered street kids descended like pigeons, snatching the bills first, then the change, their hands lightning. They beat it into the street and down alleys, bills rustling in their fists.

Apartments in Hawaii

When Zenji left, Calvin looked out the hotel window at the apartments across the way, their windows yellow and white, filled with people not visiting, but living in Ohana. Calvin lived in the Kansas flatlands, and, when he looked out his living room window, he only saw one house, and framed within he saw his neighbor the pastor and his Christian wife and kids, who sat around the kitchen table and read and prayed and colored with crayons nights after Calvin finished dinner with his wife and young son. Calvin sat in the dark and watched, the scene like one painted by Rockwell, the particular joys of a light light life. Here, in Hawaii, Calvin saw two-hundred scenes, a hive of so many many lives. A woman washed a blue and white dish. A thin, monk -haired man jogged on a treadmill. Two couples toasted burgundy-colored wine. A lonely woman stared into the blue of her tv. A man ate beer nuts. Kids ran corners. Calvin felt sad and alone, his people thousands of miles away, and his conference-mate Zenji had gone on to the big island to meet his girl. Calvin screwed off the top of the Corona he'd lingered over at the minimart. He didn't often buy beer. He stood on the lanai with his yellow beer stuffed with a lime and drank and leaned and watched. He felt himself totter, his hand on the rail. The way down was long. Calvin tilted into the hotel room and onto the white sheets, where he felt like crying. So much humanity, and none of it his. He took off his clothes and stretched into the bed. He pulled at himself until he could sleep.

Conferencing in Hawaii

written with Masami Sugimori

Zenji's girlfriend, Haru, broke up with him the day before the trip. So, Calvin had a free room in Hawaii. The two young men were slated to present a paper in Ohana.

When Calvin arrived, he and Zenji hit the beach, each with something to forget. Zenji wanted to forget Haru, and Calvin wanted to forget how his first honeymoon went, a series of island hopping days that soon ended in divorce. Calvin's current wife said, "I'll never go to Hawaii with you. That's her place," when Calvin asked Isabel to come to Hawaii with him to the conference Zenji and Calvin were slated to present a paper at, a paper on Hughes and Mingus, based on a series of interviews with jazz and blues musicians, scant scholarly articles, and a classic 1958 MGM LP that the two played over and over, looking for signs.

Calvin dropped his pack into the sand, set his glasses on a beach chair, and went straight into the water. The water was cool and the rocks on the bottom were ice cube cool, but soon his body attuned to the waves and the long stretches of ocean in between. Calvin looked towards the horn of the island, and it looked like a thundercloud, large and indistinct. He did not see as well as he did as a kid. Calvin remembered how he had gone right into the water with his first wife, Julie, a petite younger woman. He had trimmed her crotch with his goatee trimmers. Kansans not used to the beach, to the sun and surf, bikinis. His honeymoon had progressed with a phrase turned, Waimea to "Why me ah?"— a question as the two tired of each other on the long drive around The Big Island. The two were passionate white fire. Calvin's new wife, Isabel, gave him space, didn't care much to argue, was a slow blue flame.

When Calvin returned to the beach chair, his glasses back on, he noticed something. All of the people sunning themselves on the chairs had blue and white striped towels, identical—a mark, a sign.

"Excuse me, fellas," an older man in off-white shorts and white shirt said, a beach man, a hotel man. "What hotel are you staying in?"

Calvin said, "Ohana."

"These chairs are for hotel members only," the hotel man said, not angry, not assertive, just doing his job.

"Very sorry," Zenji said.

"Listen. You can sit here today, but don't come back tomorrow."

Calvin and Zenji said sorry.

"I knew it had to be too good to be true," Zenji said.

An hour passed. Another. Women walked in front of the sun.

"You two staying here?" a younger man in the off-white uniform said. "This area is for hotel members only." He was quick, sharp, his face a red fist.

"No. Our mistake," Calvin said, "we're going," and so Calvin and Zenji left the beach before sunset.

Zenji said, "Should we have stayed?"

*

Zenji stood beside the arch, waiting for Calvin. The light turned red, and people started crossing the street. A young Japanese couple stopped, and the man took a camera out of his backpack. Zenji knew they looked at him from the corner of their eyes, but he didn't care. They gave up, and the man took a picture of the woman under the big white sign. International Market Place.

Zenji turned around and saw Calvin checking the necklace stand. Calvin picked a surfboard one, then a turtle one, and held each. He studied them one by one, then side by side, and put the turtle one back on the hook. Then took it again. He returned both and moved to the next stall, right in front of the muumuu shop. There was a dress with red and white hibiscuses on black background, with wide-open shoulders. It's nice, Zenji thought. It would be nice on her. I would buy it for her, and she would be happy. She would kiss me, and we would…

To make a long story short, I can't go to Hawaii. Or should I say I've chosen not to go.

Zenji strolled around the market, looking for Calvin. A young woman talked to him in broken Japanese, with a small bottle of hand cream. He could not tell if she was Hawaiin, Asian, or Middle Eastern. She talked about the beach and the market and the weather, putting the orange-colored cream on his hands and massaging them. Her non-stop droll did not give him a chance to interrupt, so he let her go on, wondering what mother tongue would make her Japanese sound like that. When she finished her massage and gave him the smile that had never accepted no from Japanese tourists, he said, in English, "Sorry, ma'am, I'm afraid I'm not interested." Zenji found Calvin at the ahola shirt stand.

*

Calvin picked a tan aloha shirt with big blue flowers, quickly slipping his t-shirt off and pulling the sign of tourist and surfer Hawaii over his head. Calvin's body was a tad slack, but not too bad, especially for a "nerd cool" academic, although Calvin never really thought of himself that way; he thought of himself as a poet. And Zenji, a Murakami fan, wrote stories when he wasn't rooting around in libraries—and some of these stories Zenji and Calvin told together.

Calvin said, "My stomach's rumbling. Where should we eat?"

Zenji said, "Follow me. I know a place."

"Will I need to use chopsticks?"

"You might."

*

"Here you are," Zenji picked up two black wooden trays, and handed one to Calvin. Zenji found this Japanese noodle place on the day he arrived, and knew it served real *sanuki udon*. When asked how to find authentic Japanese restaurants, Zenji always told his American friends to look for names that didn't make sense to them. Forget Shogun, Yokozuna, or whatever rings the bell with you, he said, and go with Marukame, or Gyukaku, instead.

Zenji and Calvin followed the slow progress of the line, receiving noodles, picking up tempura toppings, and paying a Caucasian woman in the all-white uniform. Zenji put his tray on a window-side table, and waited for Calvin. Not too bad, he thought. He knew he was off the hinges, but hanging out with Calvin like this would buy the time to get back. Everything he had enjoyed—reading, writing, traveling—was nebulous nonentity now, of which he couldn't push himself to care anymore. But it's fine, he thought. The paper was all finished, just waiting to be read. He could buy the time to get back to normal, and how else could you kill time better than eating nice authentic *udon*?

"Like this? Calvin slid the chopsticks in his hand.

"Yes. Now move the top one so its tip hits the bottom one's." The trick was to hold the top one with your thumb and two fingers, just like a pencil, and put the bottom one balanced on the side of your palm and ring finger. When you pick up food, move the top one, but not the bottom one.

"Hmm, that's not easy," Calvin said. Zenji was worried that Calvin's noodle would get soggy by the time he made his first bite. Calvin gave it another try, but the top one went past the bottom one again. Then they caught a piece of thick white noodle in between the X they formed, and carried it precariously to his mouth.

"That's fine, man," Zenji said. "It took me six years to use them right."

Calvin picked the pencil-thick noodle up with his chopsticks that shook with effort, but held. He slurped when he pulled the noodle in.

"It's ok to make that sound," Zenji said.

Calvin picked up the bowl and sipped.

Done, Zenji and Calvin walked into the Waikiki night. The sidewalks were full of youth in their 20s and 30s—women in red dresses and black leather miniskirts, in dresses with sequins that caught the beach streetlights, and men in silk aloha club shirts, shirts with silver shimmer, men in alligator loafers. Two glimmering women walked past Calvin and Zenji. The stouter one said, "Fifty dollars" to Zenji.

Calvin punched Zenji in the arm soft, said, "She didn't say anything to me."

"Really? I was just closer."

"No. Who she wants is you."

*

Zenji wondered aloud why hookers called on him all the time. Every time he walked in city streets at night. He was not popular—though not unpopular either—among girls. He was not a swaggering macho type, nor smooth urbane type. He worked out regularly, lifting weights and swimming, but always preferred to be wiry-strong.

"And I have no hair," Zenji pointed to his shaven bald head. He was on the Big Island the day before, to kill the time without Haru, and paid a beginning-of-the-year visit to a Buddhist temple in Hilo. The middle-aged Japanese reverend saw his head and thought he was another Buddhist priest. When Zenji said he wasn't, the reverend asked if he was interested to be one. The reverend had two daughters but no son, and had been looking for a successor for some years. Just think of it, he said with a gentle smile; it was not a coincidence you visited this temple.

"That's why they always call on you," Calvin laughed.

"Ah, well, maybe you're right," Zenji shrugged.

Calvin ran a hand over the crown of Zenji's head.

"Maybe that's what they all want to do," Calvin said. "Smooth a hand over your bald head."

"You bet they do," Zenji said.

"Like rubbing a statue for luck."

"And it works."

"Man, I need some more luck," said Calvin.

"Get that hand away from my head."

*

Zenji entered the ballroom, balancing two plates on one hand and carrying a thick heavy briefcase on the other. He had picked a little bit of everything—cinnamon roll, waffle, bacon, smoked sausage, scrambled eggs, hash browns, salad and fruits. He found an open table, put the briefcase on one of the seven chairs around it, and placed the plates on the clean white tablecloth.

He looked over the room, and saw there were more than forty tables and barely a dozen people eating. The final day of a conference, he thought. People were already headed back home, or hitting the beach one last time. Or just tired, like Calvin. He had alluded to skipping the breakfast, but Zenji asked anyway.

"Go ahead without me." With a slow rustle of the comforter, Calvin turned over to face Zenji standing by the window. "I'll catch you up at lunch."

He opened the briefcase and took out his watch. Two minutes to eight. Perhaps people had just left for 8 A.M. sessions. He put the watch on and went to get a glass of milk.

*

Calvin woke slow, but showered and dressed quickly.

He donned his khaki slacks and ivory shirt and black sports coat his wife, Isabel, had chosen for him. Women were always getting, giving him things: clothes. Calvin slipped on tan socks and dark brown loafers and grabbed his conference pack.

Almost out the door Calvin paused. In the closet his aloha shirt hung, black with white hibiscus flowers, long-stamenned flowers, hummingbird flowers—shirt he got his last trip here, honeymoon of 1998, shirt his ex-wife bought, shirt from pretty, petite Julie. With so many things gone, discarded, left, thrown out, Calvin sometimes wondered why he kept the shirt. But now he knew. The shirt reminded him of days of joy, tropical days, days in the sun with the woman he loved. The shirt held that sun, that sand, that sea salt somewhere in its cotton or silk or rayon knit—

somewhere within its slick ripples that shirt knew love, Mayfly love, brief love, afternoon island rain love.

Calvin pulled the shirt from the closet, folded it neatly three times and stuffed it in his pack. He'd wear that shirt later today, once the talk was done, once the sports jacket was off.

*

A quarter to nine. Just a few people were in the ballroom, all of them done with eating. Zenji sipped his second cup of coffee, looking vaguely into the clear sky through the open door. With the drowsy quietude permeating the room, he could not believe he was giving a scholarly presentation in just a few hours. Hawaii in January, well-brewed French press in the air-conditioned ballroom, with another bright tropical morning outside.

Or should I say I've chosen not to go…

Haru would have been taking her return flight by now. He wondered how she spent the five days off she got for the trip. She was probably visiting her parents, he thought. Though tsunami did not hit their town, she had told him, it was not easy for them to lose a modest but comfortable retired life, with the tilted house and sinkholes and rolling blackouts and all. "And," she went on, "we are expecting more power outage this summer."

A caterer came in and began cleaning up the tables. As Zenji packed his things, he saw a bobbed-haired woman in a gray suit pass by his table, recognizing him in a silent smile. They had shared a table on the first day, with three others. After introducing themselves, the five of them promised to attend each other's sessions—a promise Zenji failed to keep as he left for the Big

Island shortly after. He remembered she, a doctoral student at a west-coast university, was reading a paper on "gender roles in reality TV," but her name escaped him. He returned an awkward smile, saying an unvoiced "hi," and wondered if she was coming to his session.

*

Calvin and Zenji were slated to present in the last session of the last day. As usual, Calvin and Zenji arrived early. The two sat in the hotel lobby and gave the paper a last run through.

Zenji said, "Do you say it wear-ee or weer-ee?"

And Calvin said, "Weer-ee. That's how I say weary. But it may change by region."

"Like how your father says Missour-ah?" Zenji said.

"Yep. Just like that," said Calvin. "You say po-tah-to; I say po-tay-to."

Zenji sang, "'Let's call the whole thing off.'"

"Not bad, Sinatra. Let's bring 'em some jazz and blues, wake up that room."

"We will, Cal. We will. Ready?"

The penultimate session, the second-to-last session was full of art therapists, large women in large dark dresses with big big belts at their middles—silver belts and white belts and dark brown belts. The women were laughing. Calvin asked one to stay. But none did.

The last session was a shared session, and a woman with a head full of sandy curls and a skirt suit promptly shook Calvin's hand, and said, "I'm Sandra, and this is Chauncy." "Calvin," he said back. Chauncy wore a purple sports jacket with white chinos and a yellow shirt. At his neck was a blue and purple polka dotted bow tie. He nodded, he saluted, he laughed. The four readied the room. Calvin plugged in the tape player. Never trust batteries alone. Zenji tapped his note cards into a neat stack. Chauncy, who was not presenting, but was moral support, tugged at his argyle socks. Sandra said, "Mind if I go first?" And no one said no, and so, with one quick breath, she started.

*

Sandra had seated herself beside the small round table in the front. Zenji moved to avoid the cold air stream near the wall. All three listeners were in the front row.

"Okay," Sandra said, and began to talk. Calvin took out a small notepad and flipped the pages. Chauncy crossed his legs and rested his jaw on his hand. The paper was about documentary films on East Germans' memory of the secret police. Public records versus individual stories. Generation gaps and fading memories. The lack of language in which to tell a story and overcome the trauma. The collaboration of the storyteller and the audience. Remembering as re-membering. . . .

Zenji was dozing on a long-distance bus, when he felt a gentle pat on his shoulder. He opened his eyes and saw Haru craning her neck over his face. She turned and pointed out the window, with a big smile on her face, and he raised his upper body. He saw terraced rice fields spreading all over the green hillsides, graciously curved and bordering harmoniously on each other. He looked at Haru again. She was still smiling, silently, wrinkling her eyes behind her glasses.

"Thank you," Sandra said, and applause followed. Zenji looked a little taken aback, but he soon caught up.

Sandra tugged gently at the edges of her skirt and curtsied. The three men clapped. Sandra tapped Zenji on the shoulder as he took her place up front in a folding chair. Calvin double checked the tape player, bringing the player to life for a second or two. The sound of a small jazz and blues combo rose from the speaker holes. A little staticy, but full of soul. Chauncy sat up straighter, strummed an imaginary banjo or guitar, chording. Everything was set. Zenji would speak first. He knew the background, was the better researcher. Calvin was the idea guy, and interviewed the musicians.

"Okay," Zenji said, and felt all the eyes were on him. The opening was always the toughest for him, the part before the first word of the paper. This pre-talk talk should be meaningless enough to transition smoothly, and meaningful enough to introduce the real talk. He was in trouble. With all the days he spent idling around and straying to the Big Island and daydreaming of Haru, he had nothing in his head. After a moment of awkward silence, he began.

Among many blues poems Langston Hughes composed in his productive career. . . .

Zenji could see Sandra and Chauncy's smile, and probably Calvin's too, drawn taut a little to the sudden opening. He kept on, speaking slowly, hoping to sound clear and confident. He pronounced weer-ee at one time and wear-ee at another.

The blues-suicide motif informs some of Hughes's early poems later included in the 1958 LP. . . .

Sandra refolded her legs under the suit skirt, without stopping the white fountain pen. Chauncy's eyes were fixed on Zenji, with his slow nods synchronizing with the brown oxford tapping silently on a leg of the chair. They were on, Zenji thought, and all he had to do was just keep going. Then Calvin would take care of the rest. Haru or no Haru.

Now we'll move on to a musical analysis. Calvin will take over . . . .

Sandra and Chauncy smiled and turned to Calvin, who nodded once and then began. Zenji let out an inaudible sigh of relief, and noticed none of those who shared the first day's breakfast table was present, including the bobbed-haired girl working on "gender roles in reality TV."

Calvin told about his interviews with jazz and blues musicians, what they found in Langston Hughes's sessions--what was ignored in the words, what music was brought to match the words, and what moments were lost, in boredom or miscommunication, and in a lack of inspiration. Calvin pressed play on the 1980's vintage cassette player, a castoff gift from his current wife. Nothing happened. Calvin hit stop, then pressed play again. The six-sided stars did not spin, did not even lurch. Calvin took and held the plug to the outlet on the wall, and it all moved, jerked into electricity and life, sound: Hughes's voice with Mingus's band behind him, a version of "The Weary Blues," trumpet high and quick, New Orleans style griot music. Calvin held onto that plug as if everything depended on it, and, in a way, it did.

Sandra blushed as if from wine, getting a kick out of Calvin's moment of thin ice, and Chauncy bounced his head to the tune, also with a smirk, but with that crinkle in the brow a musician has when an instrument needs you, that moment when the metal tube is full of spit, and you must play a long, held note, or when a string snaps, but you must go on without it, without that note, that hole in the chord.

And it all ended as quickly as it began, with mild applause, a room almost empty, formal regard, a quick question or two, the golf clap of academia, and Calvin wanted to hug someone or to fall into someone's arms. But he thought of the peace of white sand, as a dream, a wish, a sublimation, a replacement for lust and its extrapolation, its end. He shook Zenji's hand, and pulled a length of duct tape from the floor, a long strip that guarded a line of extension cord.

"For your broken suitcase, my friend." And Zenji patted him on the back.

Back on the beach, Calvin waded out into water with his trunks and Aloha shirt on, shirt his ex-wife had given him, black with white hibiscus flowers, their stamens up, perch for the hummingbirds, one of the only things his ex-wife left him, this shirt. One night he came home to his HUD townhouse in little Manhattan, KS, and the plates and flatware were gone, the table and chairs, all the art, the sofa, and Julie's clothes. She left a note, a kind of note, a rock she had given him that said "create" on it, and a little Episcopal Jesus with the word "trust" on his red and yellow cross. These two final things were paired together on his writing desk. She'd put them there. Trust and create. Calvin would always remember this, he knew. Trust and create. But right now, he must let go, to release instead of "create". He took off his shirt. He spread it on top of a calm wave, and it fluttered like a ray, and stayed on top, then sank like a feather does, by degrees, making its way down and in. He would beat it to the shore, by hours, by days. He would leave this thing of his first honeymoon here, in the waves, in the surf, sand.

By now, thought Calvin, Zenji is already on his plane.

*

Zenji opened his eyes as the plane heaved up smoothly. A soft female voice from the microphone warned not to leave the seat until the light goes out. He looked out of the window and saw the dazzling Honolulu sky. He sighed.

He had barely made it to the four-o'clock flight. The airline clerk checked in the clumsily duct-taped suitcase and asked if the eastbound itinerary was all correct. "Just to make sure," she winked, giving his passport back. "There are lots of tourists from your country, you know, especially this time of the year."

He thought of the upcoming flights and wondered how he could spend the time with no distraction that could possibly work. Six hours to Seattle, three to Dallas, then one-and-half to Mobile, Alabama. Then the familiar apartment and everyday routine. Only with no more Skyping at eight every morning, eleven at night in Japan. Just a week ago he logged in to finalize a meeting arrangement with her, when he found the final message on the chat window, time-stamped a few hours ago.

"I've chosen not to go . . ." he repeated the phrase to himself, and looked out of the rain-streaked window at the clouds, white and uncertain, wisps of water held tenuously as cotton candy puffs, both vapor and droplet, both there and not there.

Directions in German

On my way out of Erfurt, Hendrick puts a red ball cap on my head and says, "Wear this." Its lettering is all in German and commemorates a local *Bierfest*. He also gives me a German t-shirt. I'm on my way by bus and train to Frankfurt, moving from this little central German town to the big city travel hub. I've been in Erfurt 10 days on a sister city exchange. My role was to shoot and edit video of students studying pollution: Mercury (Hg) in the water from the war, landfills, air pollution. Reinhart kept saying, "*Weißbalance*, Kevin. *Weißbalance*." Balance the whiteness.

On the bus, I sit near the front, watch big oak (*Eiche*) trees pass, trees older than European America, their trunks like concrete, like lead, like steel: old, tough. Some German teens board the bus. They wear black leather and metal studs, piercings and tattoos. They're more American than me, seem like they've walked out of the tube, MTV. They're traveling, have rucksacks. About 2 miles in, one of the German teens sidles up to me; she dips her long blue hair to my shoulder, asks directions. I'm slow, but I reply, work toward my best grammar, try to be specific and clear. I know these 5 miles. I took them to and from the hostel every day. When the leather teens get off the bus, they know where they're going. I feel proud. One of the guys turns, gives me a look, laughs, spits. The girl puts her hand on his arm, turns him back, chortles, "*Mach dich nicht lustig über ihn. Er kann nichts dafür. Er ist nur behindert*," Don't make fun of him. He can't help it. He's retarded.

Garland Samson on drums

written with Matt Kane

I'd just played my first set of tunes with the fellas at the Mutual Musicians Foundation, the place Bird and Diz once came to let their hair down after gigs and play how they wanted. The drums at MMF were one step up from being trash cans because the door to MMF was always open. I brought my own cymbals, and was unscrewing them and putting them in a bag, when Daahoud, an old bassist said, "Kids night is Wednesday. Come back then." A wiry twenty-something sat down on the drum throne and started a complex Elvin Jones flurry. I was 19, and I wanted to leave fast, flee, save face. But I played it cool, started to mosey out, counting my steps like in a ballad.

Garland Samson, a chiseled guy in his 40s, a black man built with a stallion's lean muscle said, "Not bad, kid. You want some tips?" I'd seen Gar play before. He played so strong it felt like the walls might fall in, but tastefully, not a bang-bang-bang like Chip Masterson, but a sound like your heart coming right out of your ribs. "How much?" I said. "Nothing, kid," he said. "But I need your drums."

Lending someone your drums is like lending a camera or a child. I was hesitant, but I lent him the drums. In fact, I came along and helped Gar set my drums up and tear them down. Gar took a liking to me and said, "First lesson's tomorrow. Bring a ten spot." I took my drums home.

When I picked Gar up, he had me stop by the liquor store on the way back to my place. He picked up a case of Milwaukee's Best, lifting it like it was light as a library book. The attendant at Gomer's Liquor didn't look twice. Gar used my ten, and, when we got back to my apartment in Twin Oaks, Gar shared the case with me. I didn't keep up, but I did sip and sip, when I didn't have hold of my sticks. Gar drank almost a whole can with each gulp and hit in. I lent Gar a pair of my new sticks, and after just one round on the drums, the ride cymbal stick tip was flat on one side. He played that hard. So, that was how you played with power, with grace, with push. You pounded that stick like a hammer.

Gar taught me some left-hand lead African beats that unify the body, some Indian phrases in 11, and some Elvin Jones triplet phrases. Although I was slow to pick each up, I had a start, and he patted me on the back, said, "Not bad," and "You don't play too bad for a skinny, white guy. You know, if you love the music, and respect it, it doesn't matter what color you are. The music's there for you. I've seen cats from Japan that have the spirit, more spirit than me." That was hard to believe. Gar was all spirit and push. At the end of the lesson, he handed me my sticks, and, at once, I noticed his hands, big as baseball mitts. Gar was born to drum. He loaned me some video of him playing with Archie Shepp and Dollar Brand, something to study, from his early years. And he gave me one more bit of homework, an African beat that is a real bitch to play, but once you get it, transforms your ride beat into something very rooted, but swinging as hell. Don said, "Play that pattern until your arm is ready to fall off, and you start seeing colors." And I did. I saw green and yellow and, last, purple.

I didn't hear from Gar for about a week. Then, one night around 9, I got a call.

"Max, it's Gar. How quick can you get to the Epicurean?"

It was only about twenty blocks. I grabbed my stick bag and Real Book, jumped in my car, and went.

Gar was at the bar. He started up at once, "Thanks for coming, kid. I think you can see, I'm spent. If I ever catch you doin' any of that hard shit, I'll kick your skinny ass."

His drums were set up on the stage, a classy, but subterranean place on Troost. Black men sat by the stage, playing chess. The elite sat around round tables and sipped and watched. I was the only white guy there, although there were some chic white women wrapped around men's arms, men in expensive city suits with Kangol hats.

I played the second and third sets, kept my head up, followed well. When the night was done, the bassist gave me a nod, said, "What's your name, kid?" And when I told him, he opened a little black book and wrote it down. He didn't take down a number.

Gar was still at the bar, when we were done, said, "Max, sometimes we have things inside that are hurting us. We can't go to a gig and bullshit because we know how beautiful this music can be, and when it's not, it hurts real bad." Gar squeezed my shoulder. "You did good, kid."

I didn't hear from Gar for about a month. Later, in the paper, I saw he'd been in a bicycle accident, hit by a car downtown. He didn't recover. When I went to his apartment, no one was there. Inside, his sticks and videos, his tapes and LPs waited for the manager to bring them on out. I didn't really want Gar's stuff. I just wanted a distant rumble of his rhythms, something to follow. Sometimes, when I walk the sidewalk, I count my footsteps in 11 or in triplets and think about Gar, in his apartment, leading me through the patterns, telling me, "Good start. Now play it until you see colors."

The Naked People

First night in town, and I walked downtown to the Walton Arts Center, where on the steps a group of young men in Chiapas shirts and young women in hemp skirts played on djembes and dumbeks (hand drums) and on metal discs and tins with sticks. Many had been following Phish or the Grateful Dead and had stopped here for a concert, and stayed. The group lived in an old house at the edge of the arts district, a place missing some windows with cracks in the walls, a place a guy invited me to, hearing I could play: djembe Brazilian, dumbek with Pakistani grooves. I'd come to study fiction writing at U of A – Fayetteville, tried to give up drums, but they kept coming up; when you can play, you do; the beat follows you. "Want some macramé? I made it this morning," a white guy with turd-colored dreds said, his tee tie-dyed, his cap rainbow, rasta, woven like a hacky sack. I said, "No thanks. Want some pistachios?" I had them in a small brown bag, from the Natural Foods store. He took a few, shelled them, held the green seeds on his tongue, swallowed. "Mmm," he said. "These are alright. You're alright. Wanna party?" I said, "Ok." "It's not your ordinary party," he said. "Ever been to an orgy?" And I went along.

Turns out, five guys danced in a circle, everything, except shirts, still on. Eventually, the pants went. A mattress lay on the floor, and a girl lay stoned on its tiny blue flower patterns. Another girl sat in a chair, toyed with her stockings. Everyone had beers, and I sipped from one, from its long brown neck. The music from the plastic boom box was Phish. The girl on the mattress roused, and said, "Burge, let's see if I can make you pitch a tent," and wrapped her arms around him, took off her pants, shirt. "You a cop?" chair -girl said to me. I was 21, had a fairly kept goatee, baby faced.

"No," I said. "Do I look like a cop?" "Yes," she said. "Let me see your license," and I pulled my Velcro wallet out, handed her the card; she shrugged, said, "Kansas. That's it. You're from Kansas. Figures. Seen Dorothy?" "Not lately," I said. "Only her little dog." And she laughed, toyed with her stockings, said, "Wanna watch?" And I did, for a while, and the girl on the mattress broke away, began to dance, and a black kitten crawled from beneath a blanket and tittered and swayed and leapt at her feet. No one had shoes but me. Chair-girl then had her shirt off, and threw it at my face, and I felt like things were going to go mad, the boys in the circle now recruiting girls. No sex yet, but the music was spinning faster, louder, that crescendo before the shout chorus, and the girl on the mattress wobbled and slipped, and the kitten slumped, its neck at an odd angle. Outside a lightning clap, and rain fell in bucketfuls, in oceanfuls, in waves of red dirt, and the boys and girls ran out into the rain, onto the pavement, out of the city and into the suburbs, and I put my hand on the cat's neck, cat's middle. Nothing. I walked until I couldn't walk anymore, found my dorm room, caked in rain, cold, no longer aroused by anything, quiet, a red Arkansas riverbed stone.

Calculus II

I had always earned A's, but Calculus II was too much. I'd been to the parties where the smart traded notes on how to map the sine and cosine waves, find the points on the curves to solve the problems Ms. Simons posed. Somehow, I didn't learn it. I could sometimes pull up the graph on my calculator, make the wave, then follow the curved lines to the answers: a dot, a magic number. I was pulling a C in Calc. II in my senior year, and one night I said I was through and left my calculus book in my locker, didn't look back as the janitor pulled the metal gates across the entrances to the hallways. I was going home, calling it quits. On the way, I stopped by the cafeteria and listened to the choir. Michelle was there, out front, her voice like that of the evening call of a rare jungle bird or a bow pulled slow across a Stradivarius violin or a giant golden bell rung with yarn mallets, so unusual, pure. Before class in Calc. II, Michelle did musical impressions: Louie Armstrong, Joe Cocker, Janis Joplin. She sat up front, and I tried to sit at the back of her row, so she'd see the doodlings on my papers, when we traded quizzes. Back then, I could draw. But I realized, as the semester wore on, that a poem had more power. A girl wouldn't choose a guy by a drawing, but she might if you told a story or touched a heart string, rung an emotional note, penned a sonnet. After an AP history exam that we all almost failed, I slipped Emily a note, and she cried and hugged me, even though it drew slant-eyed stares from her chic girlfriends, even though she'd never talked to me before or since.

Michelle's voice was something I wanted to hear again. I'd seen the cool kids scale the wall to the second floor lockers by putting a foot into the hole where the Coke cans came out. I thought, although I was awkward, I might be able to do that, if it meant I might hear Michelle again. She also was not in my social circle, but her voice was what I'd wanted.

The choir finished, and I slipped my backpack on. Michelle pulled back a strand of her long, dark hair, and I didn't look long. I headed to that brick wall, put one foot in the Coke machine, and scaled it. The machine tipped a bit, but rebalanced. I stood on the machine's metal top and went over the small wall. No one there, I opened my locker quickly and took the book. I went back over the wall and Coke machine in reverse, adding a little hop to finish. No one saw.

At home, I spent the night reading and rereading the pages. I solved the problems on page 141 and checked my answers in the back. I got $^2/_3{}^{rds}$ of them correct. I searched for my errors, but couldn't find them. In class, I passed with a B or C. Toward the end of the year I found the courage to ask Michelle to a dance. She put a hand on my shoulder and said no. She was waiting for another guy to ask her.

Dead Battery

I called my ex-girlfriend when my Blazer battery died in the Tune Shop parking lot. Jawaun needed a new thick d-string for his bass. We had the hood open, when Bea got there, the jumper cables out and coiled. Bea drove us to the Little Apple Wal-Mart, and we got the battery, undid the screws, and lifted it in—and, on the way back, we all stopped and watched white ruffled couples dance through the window of the old folks home, there in the grass by the curb, Bea's hand in my hand again.

Elizabeth: a scrap of our story

"She aches just like a woman…but she breaks just like a little girl."
Just Like a Woman *Bob Dylan*

We bought a six pack of Boone's fruity, diluted drinks, and we sat and laughed. Her smile was back. Then, she cried, when she showed me the notes and transcripts from the shrinks, what they had said. She laid them out on the motel bed, and they were in yellows, pinks, and greens, pieces of carbon marked paper, the pen pushing the purple ink through. These were her copies.

There were two beds. Later that night, we would make love. It would be my first time with anyone. This is what she wanted. She wanted healing. She'd done so much of it, and here I was, the one around to do it now for her.

She'd only been there a few days. I picked her up at the coffee shop, and all of her things were in two large brown grocery bags. Clothes spilled over the top, pinks and reds and tans. She said she was going to sleep in the park, and I said, "No. Come with me." I don't know if there was love there anymore for us, but we were familiar, and a low flame burned down low, I thought, and it only needed the turn of a knob, the touch of a hand, to rise up and fill both of our bodies with heat.

Liz was disheveled, but beautiful. Her eyes moved a lot, tracking. It was as if she had been hunted for too long, and now she couldn't come down, calm down. I put my hand on her waist, something I had not done for her or any girl, and she settled. She leaned into me and wrapped her arms around my body. Her head went up, and she leaned back, arching. She wanted to kiss, and we did. And we walked to my car, I started it, and we left the coffee shop parking lot, headed west across Westport to the Holiday Inn. I had never taken a girl to a hotel before.

Really

When Slow and Haunted lived in an old fix-er-upper near the Art Institute, Haunted called Amber her friend, said, "You know, if you ever want to see her again, you really need to stop writing about her."

"I don't write about her that often, and you can tell, with each word, that I love her."

"Lust after her, you mean," Haunted said.

Haunted had bangs like black curtains, and, when she was full of lightning her eyes would peek out and flash like an anvil-headed Kansas thunderstorm on a no-moon night. Haunted, Jewish, studied genocide (mass death) and American literature. Slow, her husband, who was brilliant, and could write, did nothing. Existentialist, not nihilist, he didn't see much reason to work, and so he didn't. Slender and handsome, he could have been Tom Cruise, but he was smarter, and had wit, and was very very good at baseball, until he broke his neck sliding into third. In the hospital, laid up, Slow found books, and books found him. Slow was my best friend, despite the fact that when I called, Slow didn't pick up until the 38th ring. This was before caller ID, before everyone had answering machines. Slow would pick up and say, "Kev, what took you so long?"

Haunted said Amber was her friend. "You shouldn't write about her like that."

"Like what?" I said.

"Like that!" Haunted said.

"Let the girls come to you," Amber had said, when I emailed her from Arkansas. "Stop chasing them. Stop writing them. They'll come to you."

140

"I'm gonna die alone if I take your advice," I said.

"We all die alone," Amber said. "Some just don't realize it until they're dead."

"What?" I said.

"There's nothing but loneliness. We're always alone."

"What about making love?"

"An illusion of connection. A grand illusion. A sexy illusion. But it's still not really real."

"Really?" I said.

"Really," she said, and that was one of Amber's catch phrases: "Really." She could say that and make you wonder: "What is it I'm really saying... I want you?" And she'd say, "Yep. That really really is it."

The Djembe Drum

Jen sent the drum, a djembe, an African drum. Wooden, hour glass-shaped, with a calfskin top and long brown fur around the edges, the drum stood upright in the living room along the wall near the door. Calvin could see it when he came in, and often after a long day, he went straight to the drum and tilted it between his legs so that the air could get out and played the rhythms he learned from Planet Drum and from Byrd Flemming who taught him some of the fundamentals: how to hold the hands; how to strike the drum, the elbow and arm pivoting like a hammer cocking and coming down; how to open the hand and use the hand like a big flat mallet when hitting the center of the drum, and how to hold the fingers together, strong, the hand cupped, the hand like a taut, but flexible, bamboo stick, how to hit at the edge.

Calvin imagined the drum in its home, in Ghana. Jen sent the drum in exchange for a gig Calvin did for free. Jen read her poetry, and Calvin played behind her on dumbek, a smaller drum, metal, from Palestine. The drum jingled when he hopped his feet, the drum in his lap, a tambourine inside the drum. Jen loved it, and she wanted to give back, so she sent the drum, when she returned. She said, "The drum is a woman. Love it." And Calvin did.

One night, around the witching hour, Calvin imagined the drum's history. The drum sat on its side in the dirt. A lot of drums, 20 drums, waited. The villagers had been carving the drum bodies, wetting and pulling the drum heads, rope notching the heads taut and into place. A woman screamed in the night, gave a still birth, and the baby needed to be carried out into the night, out into a hole, and a man used the drum to carry the body. The drum was the right size, the hole was enough. No one would know.

The woman's husband was dead. But his spirit was in the child, and the spirit of the child, an unborn girl, went into the drum. And when Calvin, a skinny white guy in his late 20s in Lawrence, the blue Island in red Kansas, played that drum on that night, the child's spirit and the mother's spirit and the father's spirit came out of the drum, and like smoke the spirits circled his head, and the father's spirit went into Calvin, quick in through his nostrils as he gathered breath to play, and out through the mouth as he exhaled, exhaling with the drum, the sound into the hardwood floor into the earth. That African man was in the drum and in the drummer. Calvin fell asleep drumming.

When Calvin awakened he felt different. He felt taller. He felt bigger. He felt strong. He felt like his skin couldn't hold all of him in. Someone else was in him. He sweat and he sweat. Calvin took his white handkerchief out of his back pocket and dabbed at his head. And when Calvin ran on the river trail out back of his house, he ran faster and lighter, like a hunter, like someone who lived by his swiftness.

When Calvin went into the grocery store, and passed through the automatic doors, it was like going through a time warp. People passing him in carts blurred, their faces went, as if half erased by a pink eraser, speed smearing. They were there and not there. They stared at him, and he stared back. He wondered what was going on. The tomatoes held an uncommon red, blood red, brighter. The fruit and vegetables called to him, like sugar did to him as a kid. Like sex did to him today. The food wanted him to eat it right then, right there, like sugar, like berries to a toddler. His instincts, Calvin figured, were coming out.

Calvin went home. He played that drum. When drumming, he felt a little more normal again, like he was Calvin and he was someone else at once, the blur between them cooled. Calvin bathed often. In the tub, his body felt smoother, softer; the muscles no longer fought to get out.

Calvin never tired. He had little need for sleep. He wasn't anxious, but instead energetic, like a fire beat in his heart. Calvin wondered if this would ever wear off. Calvin wondered if he were just dreaming this, but when he played the drum he didn't wonder if this were real.

Church Teen Drum Jam

written with Jeremy Gulley

Five minutes into the church percussion jam session, one of the teens busts one of my repurposed timpani sticks. The stick splits diagonally from its center, a perfect break. Thirty dollars almost lost. I duct tape the stick, wrap from the timpani stick head--that tuft of white that I've wrapped in a sock, so it'll last--to the rounded, slim butt end of the stick. I hand the stick back, and the teen, his hair spiked up like a manga character, hits in, as if the stick had always been in his hands, as if he'd dropped a fork, and a waiter picked it up.

thddd-um-bum-bum--thdddddd-um-bum-bum... He rolls like thunder over the western Kansas plains or the 17 year cicada. Crescendos follow that shouldn't come from a timpani stick, let alone one just reworked with tape. His eyes sort of roll back, and the color of his gaze matches that of his hair. "Now," I think, "now something's happening."

When the groove is holistic, coming from the hands and sticks as if coming from the forest trees, insects chirping at once, there's little need to teach. Only watch. And guide. I play a few quarter-note triplets, move us from straight 8s into a hemiola pattern, 2 against 3, and the time stretches. I check my watch. Forty more minutes. We have time to play it out, see where the groove goes.

Behind us, a cross with a neon light shines, 9 am coming on, amber light coming in through windows. And a rainbow from the stained glass at the back. Six other kids hit drums with hands and sticks--djembes with their hour-glass shape, timbales made of metal that make that high-pitched salsa sound, and snare drums and bass drums and two drum kits. I'm hired to help the praise band make a new groove, and it's happening. Can we hold this or recreate it for church this morning? What will the old ladies say? (Too loud.) Or, just maybe, they might sway, dance.

I get the answer when, as if teleported from 1950, Mrs. Adkinson appears. Hair too big, clothes too old, make up too thick, and eyes popping like inflated surgical gloves. We don't stop playing, and she doesn't stop staring. As we play it out, my eyes close and (minutes or days) later, we find our groove--the one that we all fall into as if we had practiced for months. It's solid, it's comforting and familiar, and it's loud. Mrs. Adkinson, I think, is going to hate me. When I open my eyes and confront reality again, I see her, still standing at the back, arms crossed, eyes closed, crying.

Mrs. Adkinson uncrosses her arms, clamps her hands over her ears. She toddles to the stage. Although we've stopped, her hands still hold her head, like a ball she might drop. I play a little march, soft and sweet on the snare drum with green felt timpani sticks. Can she hear? She slows, listens. No. She uncovers one ear, the other. I have her. "Nice. That sounds mighty nice, boy," she says, charmed, and I look for the holy spirit, and think I see her in the rafters, a kind of pale blue smoke, there and not there.

I've seen, I've heard my miracle.

Turtles Are Worse

written with Jeremy Gulley

I left the gas station, Sprite in one hand, for me, and a Dr. Pepper for him in the other, and saw four police officers looking in my car windows. "What's the problem, officers?" I asked.

"Who is this in the backseat?" the best looking one asked.

"That's my son," I returned, "Isn't he cute? He's too young for you guys."

One cop said, "What?"

"Oh you wouldn't get it," I replied.

"Huh," he mumbled, and I knew I could be in for it, so I said, "Sorry, guys, gotta go. My son and I have a skating rink to get to. Wanna escort us?"

"We don't turn the lights on for just anyone," the good looking cop said, and I slinked into my car, shut the door, and turned the key. I was happy to be off, pulling out like a grandma, turtles passing me on the left.

"What did they want, dad?" my son asked, and he opened his drink. He slurped a little, and the noise made my skin crawl.

"I don't know, man. Maybe they thought you were locked in."

He took another sip and looked at my reflection in the rear view mirror. "How could a normal 14-year-old kid get locked in a car?" he asked. "If I was locked in a car and couldn't figure out how to open a door ... well, I'd have more problems than that."

"You know, the police hire using an IQ limit. Your numbers end up too high, you can't get in," I said. "They police the smart ones, send them out."

My son laughed. "Stop policing me. I'm smart," he said.

I looked in the rearview mirror. The cop car was trailing me, slow. Or were they just going my way. I turned into a neighborhood, and I could see the cop heads turn, their eyes on me, their noses pointing. It'd be too obvious for them to follow. I did a box maneuver, turning right and right and right. I turned left then and was back on my path. The fox fools the dogs, leaves behind the chase.

I pulled through residential streets, weaving through changing speed zones and stagnant houses. By the driveway of one house stood one of those green plastic turtle figures holding a flag that says "watch your speed," so I did. I fought the urge to run over the turtle, or pull over and tie him behind my car so I could drag him to road rash death. That would be a great way to get the cops to chase me again, I thought, and I could use the attention.

If one games enough, one comes to fear turtles. In Mario, some will pitch you off the screen, whether crawling or kicked, the shell shooting along the floor like a billiard ball. Other turtles stand and improbably pitch hammers at you. So, after thinking better of kidnapping the driveway turtle (though I still think he'd be better with me), I flip him the bird.

"What was that for?" my son asks, and I say, "Hate turtles."

"Shouldn't hate anything, Dad."

"You're right. Dislike turtles, especially in Mario."

"Sure," he agrees, "But those big puffer fish are the worst."

"They are," I say, "they are absolutely the worst. Is there anything worse?"

My son closes his eyes, thinks hard. "Teachers," he says.

"Bullies?" I offer.

"Yes, and carrots," he returns.

"Bellybutton lint."

"Mud up my nose."

"Algebra."

"Homework."

"And those fish."
"Any fish."
Neither of us say the police.

Try-outs, Swim Team, 1991

Old Coach Waters, a barrel-chested man, a former Olympian, told me to jump out straight, as in a belly flop, act like I was going to skip like a rock; that's how you dive off the blocks. I was new to swimming. I'd hit bottom six times before he pulled me, said, "Son, let me teach you how to dive."

That first day, I puked into the trough along the pool, the water like a small stream. I wasn't the only one. Coach swam and swam us. We could barely pull ourselves from the pool, when done.

The veteran swimmers, varsity swimmers lined up along the lane, standing on the bottom. They each held a kick board, red or blue, a paddle. And they slapped the water, made waves, and we were told to swim through, do the fly. I was small and thin, had never done that stroke. Arms up and out like an eagle, you push out and up, your arms like a birdman swooping, and your feet dolphin kick, a grueling stroke, especially for your first time. I kept going under. No slaps and whitewater down there, but if you didn't stay up, you had to swim it again. I swam and swam and swam, flailing as when I was a boy, first time in the water. "Jump out to me," father said, and under I went, like a rock, arms and legs pumping.

I made it through the waves and kick board slaps and held the edge with an arm, an elbow. They let up, the water now placid, calm. What I felt was a hand on my back. "Never seen anyone struggle like that."

Mike Fell Today

One of the guys washing the windows outside the Vista tower fell, and his harness broke. The latch didn't hold. But Mike's hands tightened around rope. Mike's body smacked the building side, but his hands held. We wheeled him in slowly, paying in line, and once we got Mike on the ground his hands were still locked, like iron. The doctors said the blow knocked Mike unconscious, but his hands held.

It was one of those stories you want to hear, but are hard to believe. Life at the site was like that, unfathomable. Miracles and tragedies most every day. My father, with an orange paint stick, wrote his last name, RABAS, again and again on the tools that were his. Every pawn shop around here must know him.

Theft was common. When my father retired, his thrifty-nickel quality came to haunt us. We opened our garage door one day and found no less than 12 shovels, maybe 20. When a job was done, my father was supposed to turn the broken ones in, but then he'd have to purchase them again from the office, so he kept the shovels and reused them at no cost. When he retired, he had plenty left. Was it theft or forgetfulness that kept those shovels? My wife said we must give them back. "To whom?" I said. "Back where they belong," she said. I couldn't explain. I told her the story as I remembered it. She said, "You're a little thief." I may be. But I'm honest, too. Honest as I know.

I thought of boys cracking the backs of turtles. Of men doing the same. What were the true consequences? The turtle rarely fights back after a few blows. I thought of my sister. Her naturalist station's pet turtle, aged 40 years, was found with a hatchet in its shell, the shell hacked nearly completely clean. Rose, a long standing resident sand tortoise, fell.

151

I watch leatherback turtles in the water on my days off. I think of my sister in California. I listen to folk music when I don't feel well. This afternoon, I'm listening to Joe, a live recording from Henry's. Joe's broke, a saintly bean-pole folk pauper ever searching for a steady gig. You travel a narrow flight of stairs to reach Henry's four or five rooms. Each seats 8-12. Typical downtown Lawrence. Henry's is bright and beautiful with yellow walls packed full of intelligencia, beatniks, and folks who aim for a taste of culture and a fair-priced drink. Joe's singing without me. He's acculturating a young guitarist who says through his instrument, "I'm a soloist," but fails to convince. "I'm not dreaming now / of never-ending," Joe sings. When I play with Joe my brushes take on their own life. The hands take the sticks, and the sticks do the talking.

"I've got holes in my stomach, / got big wings inside my heart. / Don't carry much with me anymore." There is little Joe sings that I don't believe.

You Went Out Dancing

I had our last credit card in my hands, and I bent it until it came apart. I gave you half. You said, "Let's forget about all this and go out dancing." You put your small pale hand out into the aisle, and I took hold. Your fingers were warm, like when stepping out into snow and holding hands for the first time as lovers. You guided me out into the Midwestern night, past the front door of Toto's Coffee, and we walked down the block to Coyote's, a club that alternated country on one night and hip hop on another. Tonight, it was hip hop. And when I felt the bass come through the walls and into my chest, when I heard the hi-hat, bright and quick, and the snare drum hits, rat-a-tat-tat stat as tap shoes on black top, as misery rising out of city puddles and warming into spotlight, I knew I might fall back into your arms and feel your heart through your blouse, and I'd kiss you, not knowing what else to do, but love and laugh and begin again with you.

At the Nelson, you danced. Like a rabbit. To the hip hop beats. A tall, lean black man had his radio on and his windows down. And you hopped over a small wall at the Nelson Art Gallery, your hands up at your chest, your wrists bent. A rabbit pose. And everyone that saw you laughed. I worried that we might get into trouble for the joke. But everyone loved you almost all of the time. Even me. It was hip hop. Hip, you hopped.

Stan said he'd seen you out dancing. Without your ring. I was at Yellowstone, visiting my sister, trying to figure it all out, when Stan called my sister. She was dating Stan. And Stan said, "She was out there dancing at Coyote's, her ring off, like a fat hoochie mama. She danced," he said, "with a lot of men, and not just close dancing. She was into them. She was on them. It was more than dancing she did." I went into the bathroom. I turned on the tub. I went underwater, and I let the tears rise up into the tub. My face crinkled and red. No one saw me cry, no one heard.

My sister said, "It's ok, honey" to Stan, "women sometimes do that." But I knew she was lying. This was how it would go. It was beginning to be over.

When we left Toto's, you tossed your part of the Discover card into a dark puddle. A chip of it held light, and I could see the orange edge of the card. But it was only a card, and wasn't worth much, not even worth a very long look. But I wondered why you just pitched it, let it go. It might have meant something, something beyond money.

You took off your shoes, and you took hold of me around the waist. You looked up at me with those eyes of yours, a blue that never holds water, a blue like an aluminum wing in sky. A blue that does not cry. You pulled at my belt, pulled me closer, and gave me a killer kiss, a claiming kiss, and we ordered drinks until we couldn't think. You danced with me like I'd never seen you dance before, the way Stan described. You took hold of my belt. I followed.

When I got home, I realized it. Half a credit card in hand, my body warm with summer sweat, my car empty and well-swept. I realized that I didn't do it, didn't take you up; I didn't take your offer. I didn't go out dancing. I just drove home and thought about, envisioned it, how we could have gone on, but didn't. I went home, and you went out dancing.

Pool with Dad

That summer I returned home. My father, a construction superintendent with a big firm, had left work after a break down. Some young carpenters had not taken his warning about bracing a wall, and the wall had fallen on them. Though two were hurt, they did not die. My father visited the men in the hospital, flowers in hand. They laughed at him.

My wife had returned to her childhood home, too. Our HUD house in Manhattan, KS, collected dust. And mice. We returned to the suburbs of KC of our youth. I'd been knocked down in a pick -up basketball game up at the university where I worked as a lecturer. My brain bled. I'd suffered a concussion. But I jumped back up, played out the game. The guy who'd knocked me down wanted to fight. His friend set mean picks for me. I said, "If you want to fight, let's go. Otherwise, back off," and he did. The older guys patted me on the back. I went to the martial arts room of the gym, tied a winter scarf around my eyes, and meditated. I found the path back to peace of mind slow. Months long. My young wife, a pre-art therapy major, thought therapy was the answer. Left me at Menninger's. I typed up the divorce papers on my own, using a home guide to law I picked up at Kinkos.

So, here I was back home. My father shivered in the basement a/c, watched TV most of the day. His job site tan did not fade. I asked him to go out, and he said no. Crowds spooked him. Anything with people.

"Dad, I know how you love pool," I said. "Let's go play a round."

"Billards, you mean?"

"Whatever you call it, let's go."

"I don't like going out anymore."

"Come on. It'll be good for you. Father and son."

My mother came in with a broom, pretended to sweep my father out, and we went in his navy blue El Camino, the front bumper bent in like a smile. A concrete truck's brakes had failed and rammed into my father's pick-up truck, crunching the front against something. My father just left it that way.

My father used to play pool with a shark, a kind of changeling chameleon trickster, Bill. Bill's father owned a shrink-wrap packaging plant, and was loaded. Bill inherited the plant, and although he lacked of nothing, he still liked playing tricks. Wild Bill once dressed like a priest to ride half-fare on a plane. Someone asked him to bless their meal. He did.

"Didn't you and Bill used to play a lot of pool, run the room."

"Yes, we did," said my father.

"Show me."

"Kid, I'm out of practice."

"You so sure?"

Father racked the balls, corralling the colored spheres slow as a geriatric corralling for shuffleboard. Though 50, my father moved at the pace of someone 70 these days. Before, he was full of pluck. Neighbors called my mother Handles Lightning. Father was that lit. Manic. But now, in the shadow of the work accident, his light had almost snuffed, a pilot light gone dim and cold.

Although father racked, I begged him also to break, and, after some moments of concentration, my father gazed down the path of the long blonde stick, and then pushed the stick like a piston or an arrow, quick and true. The balls ricocheted and bumped, bounced. Two went in, one solid and one striped. Father chose stripes, and, for a moment, he was young again, running the table. One ball, though, caught the lip and bumped back into the center.

"Not bad, Dad. You still have it."

"We'll see."

He smiled, his face red. He'd worked up a sweat. But he was live again, his eyes moving; his fingers tapped the table. The electricity'd turned back on.

I was no good at pool, but pushed the cue stick hard as I could, aiming at a ball right about in the center, next to Dad's. The ball went absolutely straight, hit the edge and bounced exactly back to where it's started, bumping the cue ball also back into its exact spot.

"Haven't seen that in a while," said Dad. "What the hell. Shoot again."

But I waited. We'd returned to where we started, and, although he did not do it, I felt as if my father had just patted me on the back. We played out the game, my father a live wire, once more.

Dear Tamara,

Summer 2007

It's been a long time, and I am sorry that I have not written you sooner. Just seeing you at the wedding dance made me think. It made me stop. It made me come back, after dark, once Elle and Ethan had gone to sleep, and see if you were still there. See if you wanted to dance.

It would have been a last dance. Wisconsin is a long ways away, and you may still be sore at me. I was sore too. I didn't want to leave everything and you. When you said good bye, I didn't look back. But I still loved you.

I kept this postcard you wrote me. It says "Howdy from Texas" on the front. You were on a volleyball trip. In the PS it says "See the yellow rose of Texas, reverse side," and somehow, to my high school mind, that line seemed sexual, ecstatic, and I couldn't wait for you to come back home.

I always thought you had a business mind, a sharp mind. That must serve you well up north, where you apply that MBA, sit on the city council, and are the one they call on when things need to get done. You always were so good at getting things done, and I loved that about you.

I remember waiting outside your room while you finished up a call with a girl friend. You were the only person I knew who had a Franklin Planner, and you used it. We had dinner at 6, kissed at 7:30, had dessert at 8, and I was out the door by 9. I loved you passionately, and I think you may still have that yellow folder with the poems I wrote, one a day, for you, my senior year. We seniors got out of school about two weeks early, as you will remember. You had another year. And I left you yellow roses, in a vase, in your garage. You drove in, and saw them. You said that, like a dove, your heart fluttered beneath your blue blouse, and your heart was filled with joy. But your father's was not. You know the story. I used the key-pad code to get in and leave them. But you never told your father that you gave me the code.

And so we ended. And I looked like a thief. But I will always love you, and some evening, when we both are not so very old, I hope to come like a thief in the night, rap on your door, and in my arms will be yellow roses. And when you open that door, I will be free—and yours.

Love,
James

Live at the Liberty

Chud says, "Let's go see Medeski, Martin, and Wood at the Liberty tonight." It's my birthday, and we go: Chud and Darren and me, a rhythm section. Chud plays guitar, jazz and classical, and Darren and I play percussion. We all went to conservatory in KC. Darren's also good on keys. Chud's a big, Dean Moriarty-type Italian American; he shaves three times a day. I've seen his sink, all stubbled with his chin. His attic apartment looks like a visual artist's: empty water jugs and dirty plates and brushes and paints and open books, and a hundred other half-open things. Buzz-cut, red-haired Darren was raised Catholic, grew up in a trailer in KCK, creates tunes on his computer and gives them away to new filmmakers. Someday, he'll hit. For now, a remake of *Nosferatu* plays his celestial music just under the trailer. I met Darren in high school. We played for the Shrine Bowl. Marching band. I led the section. Darren and I became friends, played in a high school jazz band, Deep Six, Darren's arched fingers over the tapioca keys.

So, we wait in line at the Liberty on the North end of Mass. in Lawrence, blue dot in a red state. Darren listens to Rush Limbaugh and likes him, while Chud keeps a copy of the Koran on his dashboard just to piss off the cops. "9 to 5ers," Chud says. "Frickin' sheep." Darkness comes, like an unresolved chord, and we push our hands into our pockets and squirm in the chill.

Inside, we're packed together, cattle on the floor. A beatnik chick ahead of us starts to dance, Billy Martin tossing small percussion instruments across the stage that land, syncopated, onto the marimba, clunk. Beatnik chick puts her arms around me and pulls me in. She's all bandanas and scarves and clothes woven of hemp. I don't mind. I like to dance and do, my feet and hips in time to her eyes, her lips, her hips. A guy with bleached hair that shoots up like a stalk of pampas grass horns in, elbows me out. Her boyfriend. I continue to dance, and we're three, and Chud and Darren each take a shoulder and pull me to the back and up the stairs and stand around me, a triangle, like the legs of a drum stool, and I'm the leg to the wall, when hair-guy comes, quick up the stairs, sees us, and stares down Chud, but Chud is bigger than any of us, and hair-guy backs down, turns and spits on the red foyer carpet, his girl gone, his girl gone.

We see her out front, the show over, and she catcalls me, and Chud says, "You go with her, we leave you." And I wave, and she blows me a kiss, her guy gone.

"Some birthday, huh?" I say, but the guys don't say anything, keep walking, tread into the purple night. Why do the guys always want to give me black eyes?

Hot Tub

We'd come over from the Tori Amos concert, straight from the concert hall, packed, full of estrogen and fire. Ryan hated Amos. Said she danced theatrics over-much. I knew this, and tried to prepare Tiger, and Tiger said, "I don't give a shit what he thinks. I'm gonna talk about Tori," and when Pam let us in Ryan was in the hot tub in his blue jeans, shouted "hey" from the backyard, while we sat in Pam's clean, white linen living room, the couches like ones you'd see in the ads for sunrooms, Pam in clothes that seemed like affluent pajamas, with flow and silk and sheen, and Tiger, with her red mane, said, "It was masterbatory, James, and I'm glad I brought you along to watch," and Tiger swayed and rocked in her chair a few beats, like she did when I first met her, her rocking to my drums: coffee shop jazz gig; I played a little too loud, but with grace; and she opened her lip-sticked lips, and called to me, "Fella, what is your name?" And I said, "James. James. I'm Ryan's drummer," and she said, "Boy, you're more than that." Our first date at 51st Coffee Shop, Tiger and I spent about 20 minutes just looking at each other, speechless, moving and staring. I felt as if we might start wrestling, under the table. Then, she took and kissed me, and kissed my neck, gave me my first hickey at 21, which I had to cover with a collared shirt and tie at the next gig; green-blue tie at a St. Pat's gig, and Tiger said, "Shit, James, it's not green enough." Tiger, with her pale skin and red red hair, was Irish-American, and damn proud of it, and I said, "Hey, my middle name's Kevin. There's Irish in me, too," and she said, "Not enough. But I'll make up the difference—in spunk and in skin." Pam touched Tiger on the shoulder, gave her a hug. Ryan came out of the hot tub and told Tiger she was full of shit for liking Tori, and Tiger said, "I know you play well, Ryan—you and your big upright bass, but Tori's a girl's player, and you may never get it." Ryan said she was full of theatre—and looked like she was getting off, and Tiger said that's the point. Guys get off on stage all the time, and we think nothing of it. Tori's doing it for us. Ryan got back into the hot tub. Pam told him to. And then, during polite sophistries and pleasantries, we all felt it. Ryan had gone under. Pam pulled up his head. He was breathing. I pulled him out, and we went home. Left Ryan to his ex-wife. Pam said she had enough red wine to bring him back around.

Dry-Mount Press

Dag shot photos of Amber, my girl, on the other side of the door. I could hear the camera go click, click, click. But when I knocked, no one came. Smirks and giggles shed through the door. Amber, naked, Dag twice her age. I worked for Dag, developed photos late on Thursday, Friday, and Saturday nights for the school paper. Dag never left school, stayed on for two decades, took a class or two. Dag smoked pot twice daily, the spirit trails wafting into the dark room, as I worked, agitating metal film cylinders, then peering into the light, focusing and printing the images, negative to chemicals to paper. I didn't mind Dag, but now he had crossed a line, taking nude photos of my girl, and then I remembered how Dag taught me to run the dry-mount press, how to straighten the bends and crinks in fiber-based paper, the best photographic paper. Always make sure it's dry. If not, it can ruin the metal press. I soaked some school papers in a photo chemical bucket, spread them on the aluminum press leaves, press open like legs or like a book. I flipped the switch, heated the press, then pushed the metal all together, making a metal sandwich. I waited half an hour. The press and paper steamed. Dag and Amber were still up there. Maybe Dag now had off his clothes. I flipped the switch to "off." No reason to burn down the house. I touched the paper sandwich, now held like pressed wood, particle board, all of one piece. It'd take some time to pull that all apart. Somewhere upstairs, I image Dag pulls Amber's legs into a "v."

Blood Brothers

My son traces a scar on my fingertip, a set of circles like Morning Glory hot spring at Yellowstone with those rings. "I have a blood brother," I say. "CJ. I cut my finger, and we mixed." My wife explains they don't do that anymore. Fear of disease.

Nothing violent, I say. I cut it sculpting, but I bled so much the older scout driving me almost passed out twice during the drive. I took the wheel of his rusty pickup truck. His face was chalk.

They had a short 4x4, and we globbed clay onto the wood, made a face. I had the nose and eyes, and I reached into this tray of water to rinse my hands. To smooth the clay. And someone had dropped a knife into the water, and I couldn't see the blade because the water was brown with clay, and when I hit the sharpness, the water turned bold, then dark red. My finger bled everywhere. The leader wrapped my hand in a towel.

The next day, we were on silence, taught to live without talk. We went into the woods in twos and laid down in sleeping bags in the dirt. No tent. And made fires. And I unwrapped my hand, unwrapped my finger, and CJ made a little pin prick with a pocket knife on the palm of his hand, and we bled together, white and black, two kids in the wilderness. Become one.

To Mow: A Suburban Cautionary Tale

The whole block could hear Stan's thoughts when he mowed. And sometimes Stan believed it. And if this were true, and if Brad were listening, he might have learned that Stan wanted his wife, coveted her—and that his wife also wanted Stan. Brad might have learned this when Stan turned a corner wrong in the rider and made a half circle in Brad's lawn, then went on to curse the world and asked Gwendolyn to forgive him. She was at the window, and her look said, "You'll always be forgiven. Just take me with you some summer, and let's leave this place and never look back at these thin children and these golf-course-shorn lawns and these manicured bushes, cut into vase shapes and squares, this tamed forsythia, and these mailboxes upon mailboxes all set into perfect rows, all their red flags set to up."

Undergarments and what's beneath are meant to burn for much more than all of this—and kisses can mean everything if anything might come of them, if everything might be lost in a moment. Running and traveling with a lover prove this. Danger always leads us to better meals and better sex. And we could all use better sex. Communion just won't cut it. The divine has always been inside us—and sex is just the way to release it. At least this is what Stan thought.

Stan got out the push mower and tried to round out the curve that held Stan's yard to Brad's. When Stan was done, it looked less like a half donut or a crop circle and more like the slight fringe of a skirt. Gwen might like that, Stan thought. He shut off the mower and went to Gwen's door. It couldn't hurt now to ask for some sugar. For his tea, he rehearsed. For his tea. Isabella, his wife, never made him tea; Stan knew this well. He would make it himself, and he would first stack the ice cubes halfway up the inside of the glass, just the way he liked it, "half and half." Stan liked that phrase, part milk and part cream, part regular and part dream.

Gwendolyn opened the door.

About the Author

Dr. Kevin Rabas chairs the Department of English, Modern Languages, and Journalism at Emporia State University and leads the poetry and playwriting tracks. He has six books: *Bird's Horn*, *Lisa's Flying Electric Piano*, a Kansas Notable Book and Nelson Poetry Book Award winner, *Sonny Kenner's Red Guitar*, also a Nelson Poetry Book Award winner, *Green Bike*, *Eliot's Violin*, and *Spider Face: stories*. Rabas writes regularly for Kansas City's *Jazz Ambassador Magazine (JAM)*. Rabas's plays have been produced across Kansas and in North Carolina and San Diego. His work has been nominated for the Pushcart Prize five times, and Rabas is the winner of the Langston Hughes Award for Poetry, the Victor Contoski Poetry Award, the Jerome Johanning Playwriting Award, and the Salina New Voice Award.

If you enjoyed this book,

please write a review!

Songs for My Father

Acknowledgements

The author gratefully acknowledges the editors of the following publications, in which versions of the following poems and stories first appeared:

"Bottle Problems" in *Pinyon*

"Band Wagon" in *Fredericksburg Literary Review*

"Sea Birds" and "Ride on" in *Time+Place*

"Bei Dao Book Arrives" and "Box" in *Constellations*

"Depress & Turn" in *Gyroscope Review*

"Up in Yellowstone" and "no amount of sheep" *Thorny Locust*

"Fire, Possum," "Dead Battery," "'67 Mustang Fastback," and "The Literary Circle" in *Otoliths*

"Debtless" in *The Café Review*

"No One Wanted Clocks" in *I-70 Review*

"Broken Down Car, Bikers" *A Ritual to Read Together: Poems in Conversation with William Stafford*

"The Next Generation of Staffords" in *North Dakota Quarterly*

"Doc Garland's Daughter" in *Caleb Puckett & Friends: In Mixed Company*

"Tortilla Jack's" and "Cheap Tacos" ("Taco Poems") in *seveneightfive*

"My words wait," "The Djembe Drum" and "Black & Decker" in *Stone Highway Review*

"Garland Samson on Drums" (with Matt Kane) in *Coal City Review*

"Apartments in Hawaii" in *Midway Journal*

"Hawaii" (with Masami Sugimori) in *Cottonwood*

"Dead Battery" and "The Naked People" in *Sugar Mule*

"You Went Out Dancing" in *Coal City Review*

"The Djembe Drum" & "Black & Decker" in *Stone Highway Review*

"To Mow: A Suburban Cautionary Tale" in *Saraba*

"New Guitar" in *The Journal*

𝒲𝑜𝓇𝒹𝓈 𝑜𝒻 𝒯𝒽𝒶𝓃𝓀𝓈

This book is dedicated to my father, Gary Curtis Rabas, who helped make a bright future for his family through his work at JE Dunn Construction. When I started writing, one of my goals was to write poems my father and the guys at the site might appreciate. That dedication to plain style continues in my work, and so I owe a great deal to my father.

My mother, Joyce Marie (Luder) Rabas, encouraged me to write, and she led by example, as a newspaper editor, reporter, and columnist. My mother continues to guide me in my writing, and I continue to rely on her good sense as well as her copyediting skills. I'm blessed with a family that values and honors writing and writers.

In my own little family, my wife, Lisa, helps secure me the time and space to do my writing. She holds down the house. A talented and skilled writer herself, she understands writing's demands. Her songs drew me to her, and I wound up being much more than just her drummer. Also, my son, Eliot, does not complain much about how I am often writing. A curiosity, he lets me be. Or says, "Are you writing about me again, Papa?"

Along the way, I have also forged some strong writerly friendships, but chiefly with Dennis Etzel Jr., my poetic brother and correspondent. Dennis has seen most of these poems and stories through the nearly daily letters we share. Dennis is a great encourager and confidant. Dennis sees, and sometimes critiques, my first drafts. He is a true friend.

Select stories in this collection are collaborations, pieces that would not exist without literary friendships. So, I am very thankful for my writerly partnerships with Masami Sugimori, Jeremy Gulley, and Matt Kane. Their stories are often better than mine.

Other friends that helped fuel this book include Amy Sage Webb, Tyler Sheldon and Alex Arceneaux, Val Bontrager and Laura Cossey, Randy Carlson, Richard Warner, Brian Daldorph, Alicia Styles, Jen Rae Hartman, Adrienne K. Goss, Jason Ryberg, and Joseph DeLuca.

This collection's title is a dedication to the renowned Horace Silver song and album, *Song for My Father.* Jazz has and continues to guide me. Prof. Michael Parkinson introduced me to Silver's work, when I was an undergraduate in the UMKC jazz program. I did a lot of listening during that time, most of it in the MARR Sound Archive, directed by Chuck Haddix. I also spent a good deal of my evenings and nights in KC at jam sessions from 1993-1995. Through these three venues—band room, music archive, and jam session—my jazz education formally began. But I don't want to forget Doug Talley, my first jazz teacher. He stayed after the day's classes were done at Hocker Grove Middle School and introduced us to jazz. He'd play a lick on saxophone, and say, "Hear that? Now play it back. You, too, on drums."

I also want to thank my book cover designer, Eric Sonnakolb. He's lent his artistic magic to most of my books. I'm thankful for his friendship and collaboration. Who says we don't judge a book by its cover?

The same is true for Dave Leiker, local photographer and friend. If it's a good photo, and it's part of one of my books, it's Dave's shot.

Thank you to Mike Graves, Donald Levering, Cheryl Unruh, and Dennis for the generous and glowing blurbs.

And, of course, this would be a pile of papers and not a book without Tracy Million Simmons, the writer, editor, and publisher who is revitalizing Kansas writing through her new press, Meadowlark. We have a lot to be thankful for through her. Additionally, Tracy did interior layout and design on this book. And it looks great!

WWW.MEADOWLARK-BOOKS.COM

Meadowlark is an independent publisher, born of a desire to produce high-quality books for print and electronic delivery. Our goal is to create a network of support for today's independent author. We provide professional book design services, assuring that the stories we love and believe in are presented in a manner that enhances rather than detracts from an author's work.

For all the debate about the state of publishing today, we remain optimistic. Readers continue to seek quality stories and writers have more opportunities than ever before.

We look forward to developing a collection of books that focus on a Midwest regional appeal, via author and/or topic. We are open to working with authors of fiction, non-fiction, poetry, and mixed media. For more information, please visit us online at www.meadowlark-books.com.

Also by Meadowlark

Green Bike: a group novel, by Kevin Rabas, Mike Graves & Tracy Million Simmons - Sept. 2014

MoonStain Poetry by Ronda Miller May 2015

To Leave a Shadow by Michael D. Graves November 2015

Available on Amazon and at your favorite Indie Bookstore...
Green Bike, a group novel, by Kevin Rabas, Mike Graves & Tracy Million Simmons

This book began as a writing exercise of Emporia Writers, an independent meeting group of the Kansas Authors Club. All members of the group were invited to participate using a McGuffin—the green bike—as the symbol that would unite the stories. Entries were posted on the group's Facebook page as they were completed, in the same order as they appear in the book. The project started in September, with the final chapters being completed around March of the following year.

"It was a challenge that tested me on many levels," said Tracy Million Simmons. "To write something and immediately share it with multiple readers, without the usual levels of internal processing—read, rewrite, read, rewrite—that my work usually undergoes was a big step for me as a writer."

Rabas, a former jazz musician and continuing jazz and Beat literature aficionado, said he felt at home with the novel's structure. "Although improvisatory, the story hangs together. It's a cohesive narrative. A good deal of thought went into the story's characters, and, although the plot was not predetermined, we knew the strengths and limitations of the characters—what they would do and would not do—and fittingly character drove and determined plot, as did the sensibilities of the three writers. We know each other, and we know what kinds of tales we might be capable of. Beyond that, we pushed ourselves—and our characters. When it felt like something (a scene, an arc in the plot) was going slack, one's coauthors would turn up the heat and test us all."

In early guidelines for the project participants, Mike Graves wrote, "We're using the green bike as a common element, and we're writing individual stories… This is tentatively titled, 'Love Stories.' I think it's the author's choice as far as building on the same story/characters, but each author is welcome to do so. I liken this to hitting a baseball. We don't know if the next pitch is going to be a fastball or a slider. Just grab a bat and take a swing."

Rabas and Graves almost immediately began intertwining stories, borrowing each other's characters and affecting the momentum of each other's stories. Simmons's contribution evolved more independently, and became almost a prequel to the story of her co-authors. "At some point I decided I was writing about the origin of the green bike. Where did this classic Schwinn come from? I was writing the story of son of the woman who loved the bike first."

As for the publication, Rabas said, "We wrote Green Bike on a shared, private Facebook page, so only a group of about 20 could see it and cheer us on. Later, we scraped the text from Facebook and formatted the novel ourselves. However, the process sometimes introduced daunting formatting errors, which took days or weeks to clean up. Later, I shopped the novel, and got a hit. A publisher wanted it, edited it, and sent a contract, but, in the end, we fell on aesthetic differences, and decided to pull the novel, reedit it, and publish it ourselves, following our own unique vision. So, the novel's been around the block. I think we can all say we're satisfied with it now. We love how it turned out."

Rabas called the novel "a wild campus romp." He said, "It's at once a love story, a love triangle, a kunstlerroman (artist's way novel), coming of age tale, wild college days tale, and tale about losing an aging loved one. How can it be all of these things? Because it's a novel of parallel tales. We're not just in one narrative. We're in three."

Printed in the USA
CPSIA information can be obtained
at www.ICGtesting.com
LVHW041800121023
760931LV00005B/135